P9-DVC-808

Depression Bums

Also by Ken C. Wise

CRUISE OF THE BLUE FLUJIN

Depression Bums

by

KEN C. WISE

———— Published by ————

Wilderness Adventure Books, Inc.
320 Garden Lane   Box 968
Fowlerville, Michigan 48836

Copyright © 1992 by Ken C. Wise

All rights reserved, including the right of reproduction in whole or in part in any form, except by a reviewer who may quote brief passages in a review.

Library of Congress Catalog Card Number: 91-51233

ISBN: 0-923568-26-3

Typesetting: The Boufford Typesetters

Cartography: Marjorie Nash Klein

Library of Congress Cataloging-in-Publication Data
Wise, Ken C., 1913—
    Depression bums / by Ken C. Wise.
        p. cm.
    ISBN 0-923568-26-3 (pbk.) : $11.95
    1. United States--Description and travel--1920—1940.
2. Depressions--1929--United States. 3. Wise, Ken C.,
1913— --Journeys--United States. I. Title.
E169.W692 1992
973.91—dc20   91—51233
                                                        CIP

Published by Wilderness Adventure Books
Fowlerville, Michigan 48864

Manufactured in the United States of America

About the Bums

ERCELL HART

Born in Mansfield, Missouri August 17, 1913, Ercell Hart and his family moved to Santa Monica, California when he was young. There he graduated from high school, became a Boy Scout and Sea Scout, and learned to canoe at Scout camp on Catalina Island off the coast of southern California.

Ercell graduated from the University of California at Davis, then joined the United States Navy Reserve. He got his wings at Pensacola, Florida. During World War II he made many missions flying P. B. Y.—Catalinas on rescue and patrol. He resigned with a rank of Lieutenant Commander.

He married a pretty Hawaiian lady and lived in Hawaii where they raised five fine children. He was a pilot for the Aloha Lines, flying inter-island flights for many years. He later became a realtor. He won many awards as a Boy Scout leader. He died of cancer February 12, 1988.

KEN WISE

Ken was born in Calgary, Alberta November 17, 1913 and moved to Santa Monica with his family. There he graduated from high school, joined the Boy Scouts and Sea Scouts and learned to canoe at Scout camp at Catalina Island.

He graduated from Washington State University in 1942 and the United States Coast Guard Academy at New London, Connecticut in 1943. He served in the South Pacific during World War II on a submarine chaser as Assistant Navigation Officer. He was in combat action in and around the Philippine Islands.

After the war he moved to Moscow, Idaho, married and raised a boy and girl. After an interesting career in the United States Forest Service, he retired in 1974 to many hobbies—of which canoeing and camping are still his favorites. If all his canoe trips were added together, the distance would be more than five thousand miles. Another book, *Cruise of the Blue Flujin*, describes a canoe trip he took to Alaska and down the Yukon River in 1936 with Gene Zabriskie.

Ken Wise *(left)* and Ercell Hart, 21 year olds,
at St. Louis, Missouri on Mississippi River canoe trip—
1934.

Dedication

TO ERCELL HART

I knew him like a brother most of my life.
He treated me like one of his clan,
With kindness, love, and understanding,
Because he was that kind of a man.

He carried more than his share of the load,
Helping those in need, a leader of the caravan,
With guiding, directing and encouragement,
Because he was that kind of a man.

It wasn't his way to get angry or ever mean,
He talked and came up with a better plan,
With compassion, laughter, and alternatives,
Because he was that kind of a man.

He never gave up, though the trail was hard and long,
Working his way higher, he would always say, "I can."
He kept going though other men faltered and failed,
Because he was that kind of a man.

His love for his fellow man was true,
Of children, he was a great fan,
A family man with wife and five children,
Because he was that kind of a man.

Contents

—Part III—

Preface

"Next our ideas ranged farther away and got more fantastic as time went by," Ken Wise explains in *Depression Bums*. With Ken the ideas only remained fantastic for a little while, until he put them into practice. In 1934, with "little money, no jobs, and nothing better to do," as Ken tells it, he and his friend Ercell Hart turned daydreaming into a remarkable cross-country trip including 2,000 miles on bicycles from California to Montana, another 1,500 miles in a canoe down the Mississippi from Lake Michigan to New Orleans, and a stint on a freighter back to California through Panama. You and I would call that a fantastic trip. Ken presents it as something you just did, during a time when, as Ken recalls, "people had greater trust in each other than they do today." And, it could be, in themselves.

Like Ken's equally readable and engaging *Cruise of the Blue Flujin*, the story of his 1936 canoe trip up the Inside Passage to Alaska and down the Yukon River, *Depression Bums* offers readers a tour through the shifting landscapes of the 1930s. America in its rich geographical and cultural diversity provides the basic foundation for Ken's story, the premise being that you learn about America, about any place, when you travel through its grandeur and distance, its small and quiet places—especially at bicycle and canoe speed. Along back roads, railroad sidings, and levees, through boarding houses, wharves, and forecastles, Ken recasts the Great Depression as an adventure to be remembered for a lifetime. He does this not by romanticizing the times, but simply by presenting them through the honest, and enthusiastic perceptions of the twenty-year old he was in 1934.

Depression Bums is a mixture of memoir, adventure story, rite of passage, and history. I know Ken well enough to know that it is also a quiet, unpretentious statement about what it means to be alive, to be animated by a sense of possibility, excitement, and joy.

I have long had the impression that for Ken language is a kind of canoe paddle, a tool that if respected and used deliberately can move you through a fascinating world. What do you think of that metaphor Ken?

—REUBEN ELLIS, PH.D.
University of Colorado
July 27, 1990

Acknowledgments

Without the encouragement and help of Dr. Reuben Ellis, a teacher at the University of Colorado at Boulder, this book would never have been written. For his help in making the manuscript more complete and interesting, I will be forever grateful.

To my ever faithful wife, Marian, who did all the typing, and correcting of my spelling—which disagrees with Webster's most of the time—I humbly thank.

To Ercell Hart, my partner in crime, work, and pleasure on the bumming trip, I give credit for some of the writing. He was the keeper of our log-book most of the time. Some of the better words in *DEPRESSION BUMS* came directly from him. *Thanks, Erce.*

I received some research help from a grandson, Greg Fry, friend, Ray Atherton, son, Alan Wise and lots of encouragement from all my good family.

Many thanks I give to John and Beulah Simms for proof-reading the entire manuscript.

Introduction

The bread-lines in Los Angeles County were long. The Great Depression of 1929 still hung on. If you had a job for $1.00 per hour, you were extremely fortunate. Matter of fact, if you had a *job* you were very lucky. There are a few people still around that remember those times. I am one.

This is a true story of Ercell Hart and Ken Wise, twenty-year-old boys, who during the depression year of 1934 made a 2,010-mile trip from Santa Monica, California to Great Falls, Montana, on old racing-style bicycles. With little money, no jobs, and nothing better to do, we biked, bummed meals, and worked on a train to get to Chicago and the World's Fair. Arriving there and almost broke, we looked for jobs. Erce found one at the Fair, and earned enough money to buy a canoe. When the Fair and job ended, the last day of October, we started paddling our canoe from Lake Michigan down the Lakes-to-Gulf Waterways System. This includes the Chicago, Des Plaines, Illinois, and Mississippi Rivers, as well as some canals and locks.

We arrived at New Orleans on Christmas Eve after a cold, eventful, and beautiful canoe ride of 1,529 twisting miles. A true-life, Huckleberry Finn adventure of river boats, river folks, storms, and calm moonlit nights were all part of our trip experiences, detailed in the following chapters. At New Orleans, with our pocketbooks about empty again, and our adventurous spirits still not satisfied, we found jobs on a ship bound for the East Coast. As Ordinary Seamen, the lowest rank of sailors, we worked for one dollar a day and "found" (board and room). After a rough, seasick trip we landed in Philadelphia, where fate and circumstances caused two good friends to travel our separate trails. Erce secured a job on a ship bound for South America, and I, after a few days ashore, signed on the same ship returning to New Orleans. It was a trip I wouldn't want to live over because—well, I'll relate that later.

I had a few pleasant days ashore in New Orleans before getting a seaman's berth on a freighter heading for the West Coast via the Panama Canal. That was a good trip. In San Francisco, after a bout with some seamen's union members, I quit. Finally I hitch-hiked the short distance back to my home in Santa Monica, ending a trip that lasted eight months and covered many thousands of miles by bike, car, truck, train, canoe, ship, and thumb.

Some of the things we did on the trip were crazy, some funny, and compared to how trips are made today, definitely different. We had no real goal, except to survive and travel wherever we could. Today adventurers take bike trips around the world pedaling 45,000 miles (Tim Young, Steve Williams, and Peter Wuerslin). Starting in 1980 they spent six and a half years globe hopping, calling their trip the "Too Tyred Tour." We had $15 each to start our trip. They had $2,000 each. We had thirty pounds each of equipment and they had one hundred pounds each, which I believe may have been a hardship to them at times.

I know of a man and wife team that made a canoe trip of 21,000 miles from the top of North America to the bottom of South America (the Krugers). Although quite an achievement, they stated that they were glad when the trip ended so that they could go home to live a more normal life again. Now people make all kinds of trips seemingly just to break records. Back in the Thirties a bike ride of 2,000 miles or a canoe voyage of 1,500 miles was probably more newsworthy than today's longer trips because fewer people did those crazy things then. Now they are commonplace. We saw no other canoeists on the rivers, and only five other travelers on bikes. Of course we might have seen some other people in canoes on the rivers if we had gone in the summer time instead of the winter—but that was our time to do it, regardless of the weather. We didn't know any better.

The Depression, a hard time for many, turned out to be a good time to bum and travel for me—at least for eight months. I went from boyhood to manhood with adventures that I feel are worth relating, and that will be of interest to people who have had similar experiences and to others who wish they had. I believe that in the Thirties people had greater trust in each other than they do today. People were very friendly and helpful to us all along the way.

If you plan to go bumming, be sure to have a good companion. In Ercell Hart I had the very best.

M. Klein ● 1992

1934 TRIP

- •••••• By Bicycle
- ╫═╫═╫═╫═╫═ By Stock Car Train
- → → → By Canoe

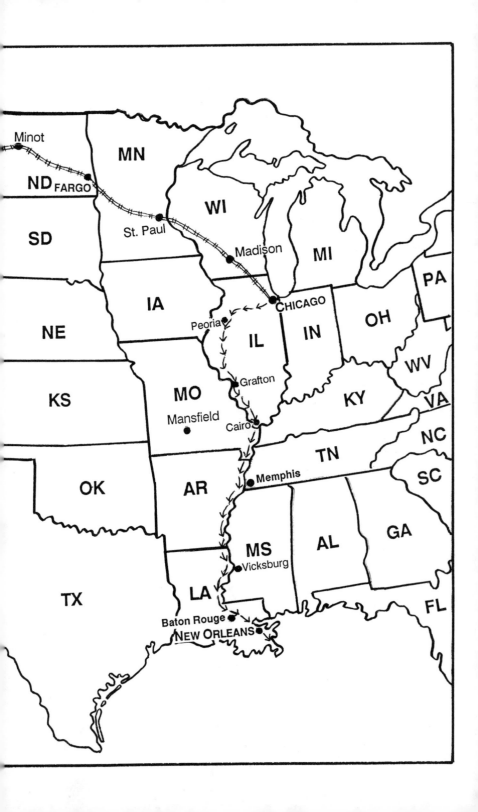

Part One

Santa Monica to Chicago
2,010 miles on bikes

HART—WISE ODYSSEY

On the Fourth-of-July (1934), we started our trip,
Six months later, it was goodbye on a ship.
We rode our bikes, Anabelle and Rosie, mile after mile,
Who thought up those names? Not me, I smile.

Through forest and desert, we went along,
Sometimes a cussin', sometimes with a song.
Uphill, downhill, and along the plain,
Through gravel and dust, heat and rain.

We caught some fish—stole apples, too,
Sometimes with meat, we made a stew.
We watched the moon, from our haystack-bed,
Comfy and cozy, "this is the life," I said.

Then came the farmer, with pitchfork in hand,
He decided we should sleep on the land.
A shower at the Three-C camp, was a good deal,
Quite often it happened, we got a free meal.

Through a foot-wide window, we climbed in the dark,
To the top of U. of Cal. Campanile, oh what a lark!
The clock struck ten, and then one more, (by us),
We better get out of here, someone might get sore.

Depression Bums

♦♦♦

We saw the big redwoods, that grow so tall,
I think it's on purpose, to make us feel small.
Coasting downgrade, going too fast,
Took a wing-ding spill, as a car went past.

On through Oregon, along the Columbia River Gorge,
We had breakfast in Washington, of milk and porge.
Crossed the Idaho Panhandle, on the Mullan Road[1],
Our bikes are getting tired, of hauling the load.

Into Montana, we crossed the Missouri River,
No canoe could we find, to continue farther.
A stock-train was available, so on we went,
Arrived in Chicago, our money most spent.

We got into the World's Fair, under the fence,
Informed by a paperboy, for twenty-five cents.
Got a job pulling a rickshaw, for money and laughter,
Sally Rand[2] was the gal, the boys were all after.

---

[1]Mullan Road—Built by Captain John Mullan, as a wagon road, in 1859-1862, from Fort Walla Walla, Washington to Fort Benton, Montana.

[2]Sally Rand—Fan-dancer at the World's Fair, Chicago, 1934. She, or her escort, always gave the rickshaw boy who pulled her a big tip.

Campus Caper

A warm July night found us, two young traveling bums, wandering around the University of California campus at Berkeley. Just before ten we came upon the Campanile, an imposing tower with clock faces at the top on all four sides.

I said to Erce, my buddy, "Boy! Oh, boy! We could get a wonderful view of the Bay Area from the top of that thing."

"Yeah," he said, as he tried the door—locked of course. Going on around we spied a small narrow window on one side which was part way open. That, we concluded, offered a way for entry. The window sill, about ten feet above the lawn, imposed no problem for us to reach by wall-scaling.

Erce, with his back to the wall, cupped his hands together in front of him, and I the smaller one, known as Pee Wee to my friends, placed one foot in them. With a little boost from Erce, I easily grabbed the window sill. Pushing the window fully open I climbed halfway inside. With my arms hanging down, Erce jumped up, caught them, and we managed to get him up too.

I couldn't see a thing inside and couldn't touch the floor hanging down. Taking a chance, I dropped. Hitting some steps, I rolled to the bottom landing only a few feet below. I warned Erce and he landed okay. With his long legs he could almost touch the stairs anyway. We fumbled our way up the staircase in the dark to the highest level. A little light coming in from the foot-wide window we had entered and similar openings on the way up had helped us some.

On the top floor in a fenced off area an electric light shone on the clock works. We watched the ticking away of time for awhile before going to an open area outside the clock room to have a magnificent view of thousands of lights. Berkeley and Oakland below us and other towns around the Bay were sparkling with lights. San Francisco across the darker water showed up like the Milky Way on a cloudless night, only brighter because it was closer. Being from the L.A. (Los Angeles) area we had the habit of abbreviating words. I would have said, "Frisco," but my dear sister whom we were visiting informed me that people in the area refer to it *only*, and she stressed the only, as San Francisco or the City. We felt rewarded for our stealthy efforts of wiggling through the unauthorized entry to gain the "stolen" view.

Looking out from our lofty tower and marveling at so many electric lights we were lost in our thoughts, thoughts of how we had managed to ride our old bikes about 300 miles from Santa Monica, and of how the next day we would start on north riding them toward Oregon. We were nearing the end of a couple days' rest from our bicycle journey, a trip that had started rather impulsively just like our climbing of the Campanile.

Bong! We were startled out of our reverie by a loud sound behind us. The clock had started to record the hour. Getting inside again we watched the works beat the chime.

We could see a lever trip just before the hammer hit a metal plate. Eight!—nine!—ten!—then silence prevailed.

"Wonder what would happen if we lifted that lever again," I remarked.

"One way to find out," said Erce as he reached through the fence and tripped it.

Bong!

"Whoops! Eleven o'clock—a fast hour. Man, we better get out of here!" I yelled. "That's a clear signal to the campus police that someone is up here." Then I saw the elevator door, tried the button, and the door opened. We stepped inside and Erce pushed the down knob, and down we went into the blackness below. Luckily the elevator stopped on its own at the main floor, and we scrambled out the door to take off running across the lawn, not caring where we were going —just getting away from the Campanile.

After awhile we wound up at my sister Elma's apartment. "Well!" she said. "Where have you been, and why all out of breath?" When we told her about our evening's activities she didn't want to believe it.

"It was only for fun," I remarked.

"I hope we don't hear a knock on our door," Elma said, "because if you're caught they'll put you in jail and throw away the key." Then she told us that the Campanile temporarily stored some very valuable museum things, and that anyone found in there would probably be accused of trying to steal them. "Oh! No!" Erce and I began to sweat, and it wasn't from the running we had done. . . .

The year 1934, half over, hadn't been any better than the year before. I had been out of high school two years and still didn't have a job. The past winter I had spent at Catalina Island as a caretaker of our Boy Scout camp along with Allan Snyder, another Scout my age. The Island, about twenty-five miles long, has two parts separated by a narrow isthmus of less than a mile wide. The one small town, Avalon, is located on the larger part near the southeast end. The camp, located at Johnson's Landing, is on the smaller part near the northwest end in Emerald Bay.

We had a little cabin to sleep in, and a recreation room where Al and I played hundreds of games of ping-pong during the winter. We cooked our food there also except when we had a goat to roast, then we used the big stove at the mess hall kitchen.

Allan and I had contracted to dig an 8' by 16' by 8' deep pit for a cesspool to be ready before the next summer's camp season. All the equipment we had to do that tremendous task with were two hand shovels. For this we got only our room and board. In fact not even that because we were expected to furnish our own meat by hunting goats and by fishing. We had a lobster trap in which we caught more fish than lobsters. If the tide was low we would sometimes collect abalone for a meal. That was choice meat, after we learned to beat it nearly to pieces before cooking.

Goats had been brought to the island more than a hundred years before by the Spanish and were plentiful, although sometimes we did a lot of running before we bagged a young kid with our twenty-two rifle. Once we captured a live one caught in some cactus. After feeding him for a few days he became our pet. Of course we named him Cactus Kid. He became an enjoyable pest, following us wherever we went. Even when we went in a canoe Cactus Kid swam after us, so we got in the habit of putting him in the canoe when we started.

The best part of the deal was that we had the camp canoes to use, and although we tried to stick to digging the cesspool four hours a day we often "had" to go canoeing, hunting, or fishing instead.

It is a little hard to believe how different the environment of Catalina was in 1934 as compared to today. We could get as many abalone as we wanted at any low tide, and now few if any can be found there. Other species of animals have been introduced such as buffalo and boar. Now hundreds of pleasure boats arrive at Catalina almost every weekend. Very few came when we were there. One that I remember was the *Islander* captained by Harry Pidgeon. Sometimes we would see this little 34-foot yawl heading in, on the starboard tack, from the northeast. Other times she would slip into Emerald Bay unnoticed.

We were always glad to visit with Harry because he had many great sea stories to tell. This skilled craftsman and sailor built the *Islander* and single-handedly sailed her around the world twice. His first trip started on November 18, 1921 and ended on October 31, 1925. His story, "Around The World in the *Islander*," was published in the February 1928 issue of *National Geographic Magazine*. Few people at that time had been so courageous as to sail around the world alone. Our Sea Scout ship, a branch of the Boy Scout organization, had taken *Islander* as its name.

Some of the members, like Allan Snyder, my partner at Catalina, and Ercell Hart, whom I bummed with later, and myself had sailed with Harry a few times. We had learned much seamanship from the experienced captain. Years later a granddaughter of Harry's, whom I chanced to meet, told me that Harry, at age 82, had wanted to sail the *Islander* a third time around the world but his family talked him out of trying it. I think he could have made it, or at least gone to "Fiddlers' Green" (Sailors' Heaven) in the glory of trying.

An occasional fishing boat pulled into our bay for the night, but we were alone almost all winter. One fisherman who visited us at Johnson's Landing would sometimes invite us aboard for a meal of his good succotash. He had a boat of about 35 feet that he kept clean and neat. The decks were scrubbed and the cabin had things stowed in their places. The boat served as his workplace and home. I remember him coming to Scout camp and demonstrating how he could walk on hot coals at our campfire. He had gone barefoot all his life and the soles of his feet were heavily callused and toughened by being washed in salt water for years.

Once at the Isthmus, four miles from our camp, Allan and I were invited aboard William Wrigley Jr.'s super big and beautiful yacht. It looked like a small *Queen Mary*. It had motor boats on davits for lowering them to the water, like lifeboats on a ship. Wrigley, the chewing-gum millionaire, at one time owned all of Catalina Island. We had our first ride on an aquaplane (there were no water-skis then) due to his hospitality. The aquaplane is a wide board pulled by a power boat, and the rider, standing, hangs on to a handle attached to the board by two small lines. We had great sport riding or trying to ride the wild board for an hour or two.

Our greatest pleasure came from our canoeing trips. About once a week we canoed to the Isthmus—sometimes each taking a canoe—hoping that some mail for us had been left at the ranch house there. A couple of times we went as far as Avalon, eighteen miles, stayed overnight, returning the next day.

Once, at another time, a fellow scout by the name of Dave (Tink) Wells and I canoed around the island on a three-day, sixty-mile voyage. The weather side of Catalina is quite rugged, with very few places to land a canoe. The other side of the Isthmus had a good harbor, but still a couple of ships lay wrecked there. The *Ning Pou*, a Chinese junk, had drifted in a few years before, and was beached in a small cove. We climbed aboard, and as we stood on her rotting deck wondered what had happened to her crew. Her mast and part of the aft cabin had disappeared. With some of the planks missing her belly had filled with gravel washed in from the waves. She no doubt is completely broken up and gone by now.

The more protected side of Catalina has many beautiful

coves with good camping places. In 1934 not every place was claimed like it is today, so we could find some private spots to camp.

We finished digging the big hole, wearing out several pairs of gloves and nearly doing the same to our shovels, before returning to Santa Monica. Needless to say, we enjoyed our stay at Catalina, but we didn't make any money to buy clothes and other necessities.

The big Depression still hung on. My Dad, an experienced carpenter, had only occasional work at seventy-five cents an hour. Sometimes he could get me on a job as a laborer at about half his wage. Getting only infrequent jobs became discouraging. I couldn't save money to enter college. Another schoolmate of mine, Ercell Hart, hadn't done any better. We talked about enlisting in the Three-Cs (Civilian Conservation Corps) which was going full swing at the time, but getting accepted wasn't all that easy. You had to meet rigid standards of poverty to get in. "Big City," eastern kids seemed to have first preference, or else there were more of them at the poverty level. If your Dad had a job you were unlikely to get into the Corps. Although I didn't try, I doubt that enlisting in the Army or Navy would have been easy at that time either.

The CCC, a Federal government-funded program for boys, had good forest camps all over the country. There were more in the western states where most of the national forests and other Federal lands are located. The camp members worked building trails and roads or on conservation projects, and even did yeoman's service fighting forest fires when needed for that purpose. The training programs were good and many boys got jobs with the Forest Service when their days in the Three-Cs ended. The results of their projects can still be seen today in some areas. I hiked a trail recently near St. Maries, Idaho where a sign gave credit for its building to the CCC in the Thirties.

One day, while sitting on the beach, I asked Erce, "What are your plans for the future?"

"I want to go to college when I get some money."

"You have any rich uncles about ready to die?"

"Afraid not. They're all healthy Ozark hillbillies. How about you?" Erce asked.

"I want to go to school too, but can't without some cash."

Finally, just to be doing something, Erce and I decided we would try bumming our way around the country, thinking that maybe things might be better somewhere else. We had some old bikes that were in pretty good shape, except for the tires, that we could use for transportation. With my mother's help we designed and made some good sleeping-bag covers into which we each stuffed a blanket and some extra clothes. We had Boy Scout mess kits and a quart canteen which we put in special denim bags—also made by my mother—along with some food. These we strapped to the handlebars of our bikes. The bed-rolls went on racks in back of the seats. My little Kodak I kept handy in the front bag, but didn't take many pictures because we didn't have money enough to buy many rolls of film. We used only four rolls on the trip. All my equipment and food weighed thirty pounds or less.

Thus prepared, and with what little cash we could put together, we started a rendezvous with destiny. I popped out of bed early on the Fourth of July, excited and anxious to get my bike loaded for the first day of pedaling north along the Coast Highway. My folks didn't seem very happy about my leaving, but were understanding and helpful to me in my venture. As I left they wished me "Good luck, son." The day was cloudy and not too hot—which made it pleasant riding. Erce and I stretched our legs and sped along at a good clip feeling free of mental depression and even like we were escaping from the real Depression. With Santa Monica behind us, the Pacific Ocean casting waves upon the shore to our left and mountains of the Coast Range to our right, the sights were interesting. I felt like I had a destination even though it was only some point along the road ahead.

While riding along we did start thinking a little about the future. The trip, only half thought through at first, began to take a more definite shape in our minds. First we would visit my sister, Elma, who had recently graduated from the University of California and worked for the Board of Education at Berkeley. I hadn't seen her for a long time. Ercell's Dad lived in Portland, Oregon. We would stop to see him and perhaps even get free haircuts at his barber shop. Also, I knew a farm family living near Albany, Oregon. Maybe we could get a few meals from them in exchange for some work —that is, if we could find where they lived. Perhaps we could even find work there to make some money.

Next our ideas ranged farther away and got more fantastic as time went by. If we could get to the headwaters of the Missouri River and maybe trade our bikes for a canoe, then we could float down the river to really explore the country. It was a day dream worth considering.

"To follow the trail of Meriwether Lewis and William Clark would be great," Erce said.

"Yeah, and it would be nice to go to the World's Fair in Chicago too, but right now I'm hungry. How about some lunch?" We stopped at a sandy beach to eat.

We knew that in Chicago the World's Fair was in its second year, and reports of it in the papers were glowing. It was called a Century of Progress and International Exposition. That didn't sound like a depressed area. We really hadn't let our dreams get that far ahead yet, because at that time Chicago seemed like a distant star away. Getting back to reality, our dreams were put on hold for awhile.

Earlier in the day we had passed Malibu where now wealthy people, including many movie stars, live in fabulous homes along the beach rather exclusively. I had had some experiences at Malibu beach in years before there were any houses there. I remember how in 1923–25 we drove to Malibu to camp on the beach. At that time a gate across the road marked the edge of the Mary K. Rindge property. An old pier where we went fishing extended out into the bay. Ships sometimes docked there to pick up cowhides and cattle for shipment to ports I know not where. Often we were asked to leave the pier by cowboys with revolvers on their hips. Needless to say, we did what they wanted. We caught many fish from the pier when we were allowed to stay. The Coast Highway through the Rindge property wasn't opened until 1928, only six years before our bike trip.

Rancho Topango Malibu Sequit had originally been a Spanish grant of 13,316 acres in Los Angeles County. Then Matthew Keller had bought it for ten cents an acre. Thirty-four years later, in 1887, Frederick Rindge, a wealthy young man from Massachusetts, paid ten dollars an acre for what he called an "ideal farm." Frederick and his wife, Mary, built a beautiful ranch house and had a good life on their romantic and isolated Malibu. Then people started coming. In 1903 a great fire, perhaps started by campers, burned the whole rancho. Only the fireplaces of the Rindge houses were left standing.

By 1905 Frederick had died. In 1908 the state started court action to condemn land for a highway. Mary Rindge fought this action for nearly twenty years. In 1923 the state established eminent domain to cross the Malibu, but Mary's small army of fence riders with drawn pistols blocked engineers and even sheriff's officers from crossing onto her property. Finally in 1925 the courts forced her to give up the right-of-way. Before Mary died in 1941 she had lost nearly everything she owned. Another thing I remember was the drug problem at Malibu beach in the early days. Being a lonely place, sometimes an ally on a passing vessel would throw containers of opium overboard and confederates in small boats would pick the stuff up for delivery to dealers in

Los Angeles, without any interference by the law. Continuing pedaling again after lunch we overtook a young kid (about thirteen) also riding a bike north.

"Where you going?" I asked.

"Frisco," he said. He appeared to me as though he might be "running away" from home. He was going rather slow so we soon left him behind.

Later a car passed us, and we recognized a couple of our friends (with "wimmin") who were probably off on a Fourth of July holiday joy-ride in their open-air "buggy." We all waved wildly, expressing our joy of seeing people we knew. Even the girls waved and we didn't know them. It appeared they were all having a happy time. We weren't far enough away from home yet to completely break with home ties. Soon after that encounter we passed Oxnard, a lonely beach which is now an Air Force Base and Missile Test Center.

One of the Franciscan Missions along the way.

Farther on we visited San Buena Ventura Mission, museum, and church. At one time there were twenty-one missions stretching from San Diego on the south to Sonoma just a few miles north of San Francisco. They were placed about a day's ride by horseback apart. Only a few remain today, and most of them, at least in part, have been restored. They were built by the Franciscan Friars and designed to convert the Indians to Christianity and teach them agriculture. The first mission was built in 1769 and the last one in 1823. Most of the converts had disappeared by the time the Americans came to California. We rode on to Santa Barbara to spend the night. Finding a camping place at Oak Park we cooked and ate a little supper, then rolled out our sleeping bags on the bare ground to sleep soundly for the first night. It had been a long and satisfying day, covering mostly familiar territory, but the following day we knew we would be in new country. We had traveled 89.5 miles, one of our longest day's runs of the entire trip. We paid for it with sore muscles and a shorter distance traveled the next day.

Following U.S. 101 north the next morning, we stopped when we got to Goleta Beach for lunch and a swim. A strong wind was blowing against us as we reached Goleta Pass, but we caught a truck and hung on going up Nojoqui Grade to the summit. We had a lot of fun coasting down the other side, passing the truck that had pulled us up the hill.

"Caught a truck" does sound strange when one considers today's high-speed trucks, but in the Thirties trucks were very low geared and would be shifted at the bottom of a grade to a speed seldom exceeding fifteen miles per hour. Many a hill did Erce and I hang on the back corners of a truck to ride in ease to the top. Most truck drivers didn't care that we did this, but once a driver tried to discourage me from hanging onto his truck by spitting big gobs of tobacco juice so the wind would whip it back in my face. I dodged some of the juice and shut my eyes for the rest, but hung on to the top of the hill. The trucks were nearly all the flat-bed style with tail gates which made it easy for us to grab and hang on. If the hill was a long one, sometimes Erce and I would trade corners so we could each give one of our arms a rest. To do this we would have to let go then pedal like the dickens to catch the truck again—at the same time switching corners so that we would be using the other arm.

For the night we found a county campground, which happened to be next to a government SERA camp where we "just happened" to be invited to supper and breakfast. SERA refers to State Emergency Relief Administration. The camp accepted only legal residents of California. I remember the camp especially well because it was the first place that I had ever bummed a meal. As I looked at the men of all ages there I realized that there were many who were worse off than I. We were seeing some of the results of the Depression at first hand.

After Erce and I washed up and combed our hair we wandered over to the camp. It was obvious by the congregation of men near the mess hall that the supper bell would soon be rung. Erce asked of the men, "Do you think we could get a meal here?"

"I don't know. Go ask the cook," someone offered. We went to the other end of the building where the cooks were busy dishing up the food.

When one paused to look at us, I asked, "How's chances for a meal?"

"Sure, with this crowd what's one or two more?" he replied. When everyone else was seated we were shown to a table that had a couple extra places and told "sit here." We had an excellent meal. We learned as time went on to always ask the cooks first because sometimes they got mad if we didn't. Besides if we asked the boss first he would usually say "go ask the cook." That way we eliminated one step, for rarely did the cook tell us to go see the boss.

There were many Federal relief programs, "Roosevelt's Alphabet Agencies," like the FERA, WPA, PWA—those two were always being confused—and CCC that helped take care of the many drifters coming into California. Some of these were the "Okies" from the dust-bowl of Oklahoma. California, trying to take care of its own people in need of relief, set up the SERA camps, where members worked on public projects.

The camps helped many people get through the Depression. Erce and I thought those camps were especially worthwhile when we received free meals from them. We offered to help clean up after the meal, but were turned down because they had plenty of help. However, after learning that we were staying all night, the head cook invited us to come back for breakfast—a meal "a bit skimpy," that consisted of eggs, sausage, applesauce, hash-browned potatoes, hot cakes, syrup and jelly, shredded wheat, corn flakes, toast, milk, coffee, and cantaloupe.

"What a Depression—give me more. I like it," Erce remarked as we left the cookhouse patting our tummies after eating until we could eat no more.

We passed through San Luis Obispo. It had a large cemetery, and we joked that if a lot of people die there it must not be a healthy place to stay. We caught and hung on to a truck up the last few miles of a long grade, then coasted down all the way to Santa Margarita. From Atascadero to Paso Robles (Oaks Pass) we had a fifteen-mile ride in the back of an otherwise empty truck, courtesy of a kindly driver.

That night we cooked and ate in the bum's "jungle" and slept on an elegant hay stack beside a goat and three other bums. Despite the soft bed, I slept rather lightly. We had stayed up late talking to the strangers. Although two of them appeared to be normal enough, the other one, a little fellow, with his continuous talk and bragging, acted queer we thought. He hailed from Brooklyn, New York, and had loudly stated, "If we wasn't so smart in Brooklyn, we wouldn't have the largest city in the 'woild'." We knew he was wrong, of course, and by his other talk not too smart, but still there was something about his eyes that made me think I should watch out for him—he could be a bit shifty. They had come west to join the CCC, only to learn that they should have signed up back in Brooklyn.

Nothing happened during the night, and the next morning we were up early, before the others, and rode seven miles before breakfast. We had met two other kids traveling on bikes the day before and thought we were ahead of them because of the truck ride we had—which made our trip for the day ninety miles. We never saw them again, and only two other bikers during the entire trip. In those days most adults rode in cars—bicycles were for kids like newspaper boys. As I rode along I thought of one outstanding person who was an exception to that statement, Big Bill Tilden, the famous tennis player. He would ride his bike to the city park in Santa Monica and give tennis lessons to us kids—what a great guy.

A strong wind carried us along on that sun-baked day. We stopped for a rest and visit to San Miguel Archangel Mission at San Miguel. We were surprised to see a well-preserved interior with original wall murals and altar that were nicer than what we had seen at the Ventura mission. At Bradley we were offered a job at a chalk mill for twenty-five cents an hour. Having a little money yet, we declined the offer—besides it would have been suffocating working there in the hot weather.

We were resting in the shade of a service station when my parents drove in, surprising us. Their little 1932 Ford-V8 coupe[1] was loaded with camping gear. Mom and Dad were

---

[1]The first V-8 Ford was the 1932 Model 18 coupe. It had a 65 horsepower, 221 cubic inch V-8 engine and was commonly called a "Deuce" (due to the year 1932). Its retail price was from $460 to $650.

heading for Trinity County in the northern part of the state to do some mining and fishing. Dad didn't have a job either at the time. We told him about the chalk mill job, and when he said, "I would rather fish for steelhead trout," we knew we had made the right decision.

There is a story behind why my folks had a late model car during the Depression that I will tell. They had won it at a theatre "Bank Night" in Ocean Park. During those years the theatre and stores in town cooperated in give-away contests. Stores gave out tickets with each customer purchase for "Bank Night." A raffle would be held on stage every Saturday night at the theatre. Prizes consisted mainly of many bags of groceries, but the Ford Motor Company got into it also by giving away a car as the grand prize.

One Saturday night my folks had about twenty tickets, and of course went to the raffle—even if they didn't win anything they would get to see the movie. That night they hadn't won any groceries and were pretty discouraged. Then the announcer gave the number for the car, which if not claimed would wait for the next week's raffle. Mother hurriedly went through their twenty tickets. The announcer was about ready to call if off when Mom shouted, "We have it!" Dad took the ticket up on stage for verification, and sure enough they won the Ford. What a prize! They didn't even have money for a down payment at that time, so couldn't have gotten a new car any other way.

We tied our bikes on top of the camping gear and climbed into the rumble-seat of the prize car for an easy ride all the way to San Jose—about 124 miles. We passed through beautiful, fertile, cultivated valleys with various kinds of fruit trees and grape vines growing luxuriously. The rolling hills had mostly oak trees growing on them.

My folks left us off at a YMCA and before they left to

travel on north I told them, "Look for us at your camp and be sure to have some fish for us to eat."

"We'll watch for you all right," Dad said as the little Ford took off.

We blew ourselves to a room at the "Y." We wanted to clean up because the next day we expected to reach Berkeley where my lovely sister lived. We didn't want her to be too much ashamed of us bums. She might not take us in, or worse, not feed us. After a swim and a hot shower we rested well in our soft beds—what a difference from the hard ground. Pads or air mattresses, we had none.

In the morning after pedaling about 20 miles we stopped to visit San Jose de Guadalupe Mission, built in 1797, which had been mostly reconstructed—then headed on north. We were traveling the Camino Real (Royal Road) of the Franciscan Friars, and the Mission had been one of their stopping places. The next and last one was at Sonoma beyond Frisco. Along the way we enjoyed eating excellent plums from orchards on both sides of the road. Now that area is all towns. About fifty miles farther and some tough pedaling, we arrived at Elma's apartment. Sis greeted us happily, surprised, because like she said, "I didn't think you would really get this far on your old bikes." That evening after supper Erce and I went to visit the University of California campus. . . .

For some time we listened for the sound of footsteps in the hall, but luckily no police knocked on our door—so about midnight we relaxed enough to unroll our sleeping-bags on the floor to get some rest. Before we dozed off Erce confided in me he had seen some crates of big bones in the Campanile. We rested uneasily that night, but in the morning were bright and cheery.

I joshed Elma. "Erce and I consider the U. of C. campus very beautiful and would give it a first class rating except that it is not too well policed."

"A good thing for you that it isn't," she retorted. We laughed. We were not only well fed and rested, we were un-arrested—and we already had traveled, with our old bikes, 296 miles on a trip that had really just started.

Mining and Fishing

We took a day off from traveling to wash our clothes and to clean and oil our bikes for the trip on north to Oregon. Rosie's rear tire leaked air, so Erce took her to a bike shop to get a shot of Neverleak put in the tube. This liquid, gooey-looking stuff usually stopped a leak.

Somewhere along the way we had started to call our bikes by name—Rosie for Erce's, and Anne or Anabelle for mine. How we came by these names I don't remember, but we must have thought of our bikes as live steeds. The names stuck until the end of the trip. We had fun with some expressions like, "I'll take Rosie to town to get bread," or "Watch Anne for me, I wouldn't want her to run off with some other guy while I'm gone."

On July 10th, starting our second week, we gave Elma our good-byes and thank-yous for putting up with us, then caught the ferry *Golden Poppy* to go across the bay to San

Francisco.

"Good luck, you'll need it." Sister's parting words rang in my ears as I looked ahead to what I thought would be yet greater adventures.

On shore we rode our bikes along the Embarcadero. This three-and-a-half mile, crescent-shaped street is edged with piers and wharves, including Fisherman's Wharf, famous for seafood restaurants. We rode on to Golden Gate Park, on the west side, where we visited the aviary, aquarium, natural history and memorial exhibits. Elma had told us, "Be sure to visit Golden Gate Park." There were paintings, ship relics, and many other things that were all new and very interesting to us. The park extended four miles with walks and gardens of great beauty. We couldn't see it all without extending our stay, but we saw enough to know it was a worthwhile visit. At noon we spread our wares on the lawn to eat and rest.

Our little food sacks were handy, because we could have a meal wherever we happened to be at lunch time. Of course we had to keep restocking them with food about every other day. Mid-day meals usually consisted of raisins—six cents a pound—nuts, chocolate, cheese, and bread, which at that time cost eight cents a loaf.

After satisfying our hunger, we rode down to the ferry landing where the *Mendocino* had just docked. We wheeled our steeds aboard for her return trip to Sausalito. On the way we passed very close to the new Federal penitentiary on Alcatraz Island, a foreboding looking place. The prison is now obsolete and not in use. Alcatraz is famous for never having had a prisoner escape, although many have tried. There may be a couple of prisoners unaccounted for, but the assumption is that they perished in the cold water of San Francisco Bay. I can believe that. The Golden Gate Bridge was in the planning stage, but not yet started. I saw it in 1936 when just the towers were up.

In the evening we were on our bikes riding somewhere between San Rafael and Novato. Sighting a haystack in a field, we figured it would be a good spot to spend the night— except that we would have to forgo a campfire because of the fire danger—so we had a cold supper. We had made only forty-seven miles, but had enjoyed two ferry rides and had seen many sights, including a parade of Knights Templar in Frisco. (Sorry, Elma.) We could keep accurate mileage because my bike had a cyclometer on the front wheel. However we had to remember to write down the total mileage at the end of each day in our log-book. Erce usually kept the record of our day's events, or if he was cooking supper, I might do it. Very few of our days were uneventful.

The next morning we rode ten miles before stopping for breakfast. We enjoyed getting up early to ride in the cool of the day. The weather had been getting hotter and reached 105° F. that day. When we started again I found that one of Anne's tires had lost most of its air—so we walked about a half mile to a service station to fill it. At Santa Rosa I had some much needed Neverleak put in the tube to stop the leak—this being much cheaper than buying a new tube. Sometimes when we had tire trouble someone in a car would stop to offer us the use of a pump, which was pretty much standard equipment in those days.

For lunch we had apples, plums, and watermelon. We stopped at Geyserville for a siesta, for the weather was exhaustingly hot. Instead we changed a tire for two Wisconsin women for whom we felt sorry. They offered us a slice of watermelon, but we were already full and spitting seeds. The smoke from a forest fire near Cloverdale, ahead of us, clouded the sun—which looked like a blood-red ball. We pedaled along as ashes fell around us, on past fields of grape vines and the Asti—Italian Swiss Colony Winery, which is still operating today. They give tours of their plant and have a wine-tasting room, where visitors can have free tastes of their wines.

North of Cloverdale the air cleared as we rode along a new road beside the Russian River. Near Healdsburg we saw some people swimming in a pool behind a dam. We found some willows where we could change into our trunks to join the swimmers. Seldom did we pass up an opportunity to have a swim to cool off a bit. Unfortunately this time Erce cut his foot on a platform float and we had to bandage the cut to stop the bleeding. He could still pedal his bike without much pain. Toward evening we found a place beside a small stream to camp. We had made sixty-three miles that day and still had time to meet, at the swimming hole, some nice Italian people who worked in the grape fields.

The next day we reached Ukiah about lunch time. We found a campground where we could take a shower—which almost cost us twenty-five cents, but we talked our way out of paying. Ukiah had well kept-up homes with shady streets, and appeared to me to be a place where I might like to live some day. The weather hadn't cooled off any as we left town. We were really hot going up the grade south of Willits when a hog truck came along. The driver slowed down and yelled, "You fellows want a lift?" "Sure do," we responded, so with Anne and Rosie aboard we rode the smelly truck eleven miles to town. We had been glad to get into the truck, and also glad to get out.

We were getting into stands of tall timber, with little green meadows and rail fences to keep the cattle and horses off the road. At Laytonville we bought bread and a steak, then camped four miles past the village to have our supper of steak smothered in onions with some toast. We really splurged that night to make up for a couple of days without meat to eat. We had pedaled only thirty-six miles, but had gone farther because of the hog-truck ride.

We slept well on a gravel bar and were awakened to the quacking of ducks on the creek, which we later learned had the name of Rattlesnake. Luckily we hadn't seen any snakes. The name reminded me of one camp I had made on Catalina where there were many rattlesnakes. I had lifted a big rock to make a fireplace, and there coiled under it lay a big rattlesnake. I dropped the rock and ran. I chose a different place to camp that night.

Friday the 13th started with a bang! Anne's front tire blew out, cut on a sharp rock. We patched it, borrowed a pump to inflate it, and traveled on. We had acquired a tube patching-kit by that time, because of so much trouble before with the old tires and tubes. Our bikes were a racing type with small, narrow tires about half worn out. They had coaster brakes, as hand brakes hadn't shown up yet, and of course only one gear. No bikes had more at that time. We had the handle-bars turned up so that we could ride in a more comfortable upright position. During the afternoon our road wound through great groves of big redwood trees and beside rivers which made for very pleasant biking. At our slow pace we had time to see much more than people speeding by us in cars. It was easy for us to hop off our bikes to go see a waterfall, a special tree, or perhaps watch a deer as it escaped up a hillside. When we came to the Eel River we stopped for a swim. Erce had to keep his sore foot out of the water, but he managed quite well.

The state of California had many of the finest redwood groves protected as preserves. We visited the tallest one-room house in the world—a giant redwood which had been burned out in the center. It contained a door and two windows and a twenty-five foot round room, that had been made into a gift shop. It was the biggest tree I had ever seen. The large size and great age of the redwoods made me feel small and insignificant.

We camped at Richardson's Grove where a kind lady gave us string-beans, tomatoes, and fresh bread for our supper. We took in the special campfire entertainment in the evening. Because of our swim and sight-seeing, we made only thirty-nine miles all day.

We had a bad road for seven miles the next day, because of construction work on it. My bike tire needed pumping every few miles. I needed to get some more Neverleak when we came to civilization again. At Dyerville Flat we saw the tallest known tree, a 364-foot redwood *(Sequoia sempervirens)* with a thirteen-foot diameter at chest height. It seemed to tower to the clouds as I bent over backwards to look up at its top. It was a magnificent specimen.

About five that day we were lucky to arrive at a Three-C camp where we bummed our supper. The cook fed us really great and then handed us a bag of doughnuts to take along. Earlier we had stopped to pick all the blackberries we had containers for at a wild patch along the road. We waded through the bushes in our short pants, which didn't protect our legs from the sharp thorns. Finding a very nice camping place about a mile beyond the Three-C camp we pulled off the road, leaned our bikes against a redwood, and made camp. We had had our supper and had already planned our breakfast of blackberries and doughnuts so rested around a campfire.

Ercell carried a fishing line and hooks and tried several times during the trip to catch fish, but never did have any luck. He used a little dough-ball for bait and a willow or whatever he could find near camp for a fish pole. Although our meals weren't what one would call a balanced diet, we got by most of the time, having enough food to satisfy and keep us healthy. A few times we had only beans for supper, and for breakfast only prunes that had been put to soak the night before.

July 15th we made it to Eureka, where I had Anne's front tire fixed. The post office didn't have any mail for us—so we went on to Arcada, where we stocked up on a few groceries. About five miles farther we found a campsite on the bank of the Mad River. Erce went fishing while I built a fire and cooked our supper, then he washed dishes afterwards, while I tried fishing—no luck. We had what we considered a good day's run of sixty miles with a grand total of 586 miles showing on Annabelle's cyclometer.

The next day we started a side trip inland toward Weaverville in Trinity County. We had caught onto the tailgates of trucks going up two big hills and had great downhill rides before Mom Wise came up behind us in her car and gave us a lift to their camp on New River just past a place called China Creek, and up a road toward Denny.

Happily we greeted our friend, Allan Snyder (my Catalina Buddy). "Hi, Al. Finding any gold?" I asked.

"Hi, guys. You finally made it. What took you so long?" he asked, ignoring my question.

"We had too many flat tires," Erce jokingly told him.

Al's parents and mine were camping together and trying their luck mining. We were all up early the following morning. After breakfast we packed a lunch, took along some gold-pans and fishing poles—provided by my dad—and hiked several miles down the New River to their mining operations. We helped to lower a sluice box down a steep bank to the river. Then tried our luck with the gold-pans and sluicing all morning, finding several large flakes of gold but not enough to keep us at the hard work.

"I'll show you guys a good swimming hole," Allan told us after lunch.

Erce said, "I want to go fishing."

"I'll go with you, Al. I'm ready for a swim." So while Erce and our fathers went fishing, Al and I retreated to the "ol' swimmin' hole." The river had washed out a fifty-foot basin in the rock in years past that made a natural round pool. We dove in and floated around and around with the current which wasn't very strong that late in the summer. What a wonderful, relaxing time we had—forgetting the Depression and the rest of the world, neither of which were on my mind anyway, because I was just living one day at a time.

Erce had caught the first fish and I found the first flake of gold, which made us both happy. We returned to camp with a good mess of small trout for a hearty meal which we ate around a campfire. We didn't catch any of the big steelhead trout—the rainbows that go to sea for a couple of years, returning up the river where they were born to spawn. They come back in the fall weighing from five to twenty-five pounds, and are a real prize to catch. It had been a friendly, satisfying day, and continued so for a couple more. We took a trip up the North Fork of the Trinity River where lots of placer mining was taking place. With high pressure hoses, men were washing the red soil banks through their sluice boxes, making the river muddy and spoiling the fishing. Piles of rock were tell-tales that a creek had been worked over for

— MINER'S CABIN — TRINITY RIVER — TRINITY CO., CALIF. —

Miner's cabin—Trinity River—Trinity County, California

the elusive yellow gold. It seemed like every creek, big or small, had a miner—or would-be miner—digging for a living, and very few making it. Many people staked mining claims, did the required assessment work—or claimed they did—just to have a place to live. They would fish and hunt to get by all year one way or another. For many it was a way to survive the Depression and better than standing in bread lines. Some lived in shacks, while others built respectable cabins and more or less retired there.

I knew of one enterprising young man, by the name of Bud Schell, who made his living during the Depression years by driving a truck loaded with supplies of all kinds back into the mountains wherever there were miners needing his wares. He had a variety store on wheels that included food, clothes, gloves and sundries that otherwise would be hard to come by for people living along the many creeks.

Bud had a regular schedule so that people knew the day and approximate time when he would come to their location. Some miners hiked several miles from their claims to be on the road when Bud's truck arrived. One item that sold well was salt for both human and animal consumption. Most of the people that lived far back from the road had a horse or two or maybe just a donkey. One man I heard about lived ten miles from the end of the road and owned a pair of mules— one to ride and one to pack.

If Bud didn't happen to have what someone wanted he would take an order and bring it on his next trip. Sometimes he had embarrassing shopping to do, as you can imagine, for not all of the miners were men. Also some men had their wives with them or sent them to do the buying. Some of Bud's customers, not having ready cash, would pay for their purchases with gold dust. Not knowing about gold values by weight and not having a scale, Bud took the miner's estimate of his pinch of gold—sometimes adding a little or taking some back—to pay for his order. When the gold was turned in at the bank, the cash received for it was never off more than a few cents, one way or the other, for the cost of the purchase. That said a lot for the miner's honesty and good judgment.

One of Bud's regular customers was a mentally deficient man who lived alone in a cabin near the road. It was thought that he had been put there by his relatives to keep him out of their way and so he wouldn't embarrass them. This fellow had a large jar of silver coins, supplied by his relatives, that he left on his kitchen table. He didn't understand money values so to pay for his purchases the jar was handed to Bud to take out what was owed. Before the Fourth of July he'd order a cherry pie. When it came he would run Old Glory up

Erce (left) and Ken at cave and camp at
Canyon Creek Lake in Trinity Alps.

a pole, eat the pie and in that way celebrate the Day of Independence. He had a pretty good life so maybe wasn't all that dumb after all.

On one trip to this fellow's place, Bud had brought his bride of a few weeks along with him. They were surprised and embarrassed to find their customer coming to the truck wearing nothing but a pair of "long johns" which looked like they had been worn night and day for some time. Bud's wife didn't budge from her seat, while he waited on the strangely dressed man.

The early day miners in this and other areas had had Chinamen shipped in from China to work in the mines and creeks at very low wages. Even so, many of the Chinese saved enough money in a few years to return to China to live well for the rest of their lives, so I have heard. Some, however, chose to stay in California and go into business. Weaverville had several Chinese families living there when I visited there in the Thirties.

Up the North Fork of the Trinity River, a couple of miles from the road, lived an elderly (about ninety) Chinese lady. She grew a large garden and was nearly independent of the world. She seldom came out of her isolation for any reason. Once on a visit to see her I noticed that she grew opium poppies in her garden, but then many of the Chinese had pots of opium shipped to them from China to use in their pipes. Neighbors of the old lady would check on her from time to time. The last time they did, she was found dead in her bed with her false teeth lodged in her throat. Evidently she had choked to death on her own teeth.

Bud met many different types of people during his time with the traveling store—good, bad, funny, strange and indifferent—and he beat the Depression while doing it.

On July 21st we moved camp up Canyon Creek a mile or so past Dedrick, an old mining district. We decided to hike to Canyon Creek Lakes in the beautiful Trinity Alps country.

Depression Bums

◆◆◆

After rigging up some pack-boards we loaded our sleeping bags and some food and hiked the twelve miles to the first lake, through green forested country beside a clear creek. We could see high, jagged ridges ahead. We caught four nice trout for supper, and shared two of them with a weasel—his decision, not ours. A coyote yapped nearby as we made our beds of boughs in a rock cave near the lake. We had plenty of food because a party leaving the lake gave us some of theirs that they didn't want to carry back.

Ercell had studied geology so he explained to me how the lakes had been dug out by a glacier and showed me some polished granite rocks smoothed by the ice moving over them. The next day we hiked to the upper lake and back, did some more fishing, and took it easy. That night the nearly full moon shining on the whitish rocks looked like a covering of snow.

Erce and I agreed we should continue our bike trip soon, because our hearty appetites were diminishing our benefactors' food supply. Allan and my folks arrived at the lake as we were preparing to leave. They encouraged us to stay, but as hard as it was to leave, we did so. By the time we got back to the base camp Erce's sore foot that he had cut on the swimming hole float was giving him a lot of pain—his shoes were about worn out. After cleaning the sore, he lanced it, releasing the pressure and relieving some of the pain. We washed all our duds except what we had on, then visited the quaint old town of Dedrick with its antique post office and stores that appeared to have been built in the last century when the miners first came to that part of the country.

July 27th, after a good breakfast provided by Allan's Mom and Dad, we rolled our bikes out for a rough ride on a rocky road to Junction City. My bike's front tire blew out for the third time about five miles before we got there, so I had to walk to town to get it fixed. We were heading west toward the Coast Highway (101) that we had left twelve days before, at one point walking four miles over road construction before getting to a paved road again. Later in the day our luck changed for the better because we had a lift in a government truck to a Three-C camp at Hawkin's Bar where we were invited to stay.

After a refreshing shower there we approached the cook house, where we were treated to a good meal even though the others had already finished eating. After supper we went a mile beyond the CCC camp before finding a spot to bed down for the night. The fifty-one hard miles we traveled that day made us tired so we rested well. We would camp most anywhere there was water for washing.

We rode until we found a berry patch before stopping for breakfast the next morning. The road along the frolicking Trinity River took us up and down grade a lot. We caught a tow up a five mile grade and coasted down four miles, then hooked on to the same truck on the next hill. The truck driver said, "I clocked you at thirty-three miles per hour going down that last hill."

"Wow! That's pretty fast for these old bikes," I shouted back. I think it was a good thing the plug in Anne's front tire didn't blow on that down hill, otherwise I might have taken a bad spill. We picked berries and apples along the roadside for our lunch. Past Blue Lake we camped in the same place we did two weeks before on the Mad River five miles out of Arcata. We had made a big scenic and worthwhile loop, but were again on our own, and off to Oregon.

The next day we rode along the Coast Highway past many lagoons formed by sand bars between them and the ocean. We walked up several hills and coasted down the other sides through redwood and fir forests. Wild, sweet blackberries which we never tired of were again our fare for lunch. The road followed Prairie Creek through pretty, fern covered hills.

At a Three-C camp we cut wood to earn our supper—

plus a bag of fruit. Not very often did we have to work for a meal. In fact I can think of only one other time, at a government camp, that we did, and then we washed some pots and pans after eating. We rode until late evening before we found a deserted side road to go up a little way to camp beside a clear creek among the big trees. With our pocket knives we cut bunches of bracken ferns for our beds to keep them above the damp ground. We had made an exact average day's run of fifty-three miles, and were about that much farther north.

The light rain in the morning made it difficult for us to get out of warm bags, shake the water from them, and build a fire. Although we didn't have a tent, our sleeping bags were water-proofed and kept us dry many nights during rainy spells. Before we left home we had coated our bag-covers, a finely woven duck material, with paraffin that had been melted in hot coal oil—painting on two coats. Each bag had a little hood over the head that could be staked up like a small tent about two feet high. Also a pocket was made the full width of the bag at the head in which we kept extra clothes to use as a pillow. I have never had a better bag for roughing it. The coal oil smell even wore off after awhile. They were a little stiff during the cold weather—of which we saw plenty later on—but the bags served us well for the entire trip. One wool blanket and a flannel sheet made up the inside lining.

After breaking camp we rode for several hours in the rain. Finally after coasting down a long hill to the ocean we broke out of the clouds into clear weather. The big waves thundered on the rocks along the shore, showering sprays of white foam high in the air above them. Farther along we crossed the Klamath, a large river for California. We were making good time and soon saw Crescent City ahead in the distance. The half-round bay had many white buildings along its shore sparkling in the bright sunlight. When we arrived there it didn't take us long to locate the post office. The letters we received from people back home were eagerly read. Then we went to the beach where we took a couple hours off traveling to answer our mail. We wanted our friends to know that Portland, Oregon would be the place for them to write to us next and that we were about to leave California.

We bought a few new spokes for Rosie's rear wheel, which had started to wobble a bit, and put them in at a service station where we could get air to inflate the tire. Next, we found a grocery store to refill our near-empty food bags. Into them went bread, butter, bologna, oatmeal, cheese, two cans of fish, and some rice. With our larder stocked we rode out of town towards Grants Pass on U.S. 199, back into the mountains.

We camped on the bank of Smith River, a large clear river with no fish. I say, "no fish," only because we couldn't catch any. We knew that our angling ability would not supply us with food. That is why we bought the canned salmon, at least it wouldn't "get away."

Our run for the day equaled forty-two miles, and we had pedaled a distance of 803 miles from Santa Monica—recorded on my cyclometer. Thus for the fifteen traveling days we had averaged fifty-three and a half miles per day. For the twenty-seven days we had been bumming, we had spent $2.28 for food, and other costs such as a room at the "Y," ferry rides, and Neverleak for bike tires came to $2.78 for a grand total of $5.06. At that rate we figured we could travel on for a couple more months with the money we had left—if our luck in finding CCC camps at supper time continued about the same. These were our calculations around a campfire on July 30th, our last day in California for many months. We had no idea at that time where we would end up, except that we were thinking "Missouri River and a canoe."

3

Oregon

We followed the Smith River until it became a small creek. The highway led us through beautiful forests beside clear pools and lively rapids in other places. We went by several small sawmills being worked in the woods. We worked hard pedaling uphill all the way from the coast to the Siskiyou Summit—nearly forty-five miles. About three miles from the top we crossed the state line into Oregon—good-bye California and hello to the Beaver State.

Our first accident occurred as we were coasting down grade. Erce, ahead, was making a sweeping curve to the right when an uphill bound car forced him over into the gravel. His bike slid and he went head-over-bicycle, rolling and sliding in the fine rocks beside the pavement. I fortunately had more time to brake hard and keep out of the way of the car, whose driver never bothered to stop. Because of the hot weather, we were wearing only shorts. When I got to my partner to help him he looked like he had rolled in thorny blackberry vines. Blood appeared in spots all over him. His knees, shoulders, and forehead had taken the worst of the fall because they were the points that hit gravel as he rolled over and over. The rolling and not hitting anything, other than the ground, had kept him from having any broken bones.

"Man! For a second I thought you were a goner."

"So did I!" Erce said as he got to his feet with a little help from me.

"That darn car forced you right off the road."

"It was my fault for being on the wrong side," Erce admitted.

Some friendly people in another car stopped to help us clean his abrasions and paint them with Mercurochrome. I picked Rosie up, finding that she hadn't suffered as much damage as Erce, and after I straightened her handlebars, appeared more ready to go than her rider. Erce limped along for a little while, but soon got on his bike to ride again. "You can't keep a good Scout down," I told him. When we got to Elk Creek we were much in need of a swim and bath, which we enjoyed after our long ride.

Late in the afternoon we stopped at a farm and asked the farmer if he would sell us some fresh corn from his garden. "Nope, but I'll give you some," he said. While he picked a half dozen ears, his wife came out of the house with a loaf of freshly baked bread and handed it to us.

"With our blessing," she said. They wouldn't even accept our offer to do some work. What wonderful, generous people we met all along the way. We camped on the bank of the Illinois, a river whose clear water we didn't hesitate to drink. In fact, we drank water from any creek or river if it looked clean, and without any ill effects.

Our first day in Oregon was memorable for an accident that could have ended our trip, but didn't, and the first night we remembered for having sweet corn and fresh bread around a campfire. We camped only one half mile from the road junction that lead to the Oregon Caves—now a National Monument. When we saw the sign to the caves and found that they were only twenty miles from the highway, we headed that way. It would mean only an extra day of our time, and what was time to us anyway? It surely wasn't money. Much of the road turned out to be a 6% uphill grade, but luckily we got a tow up the last eight miles of it.

Through a natural opening we entered the cave, a series of beautiful marble and limestone rooms separated by small passages. It took two hours to walk the one and a half mile trail, illuminated by electric lights, to the man-made tunnel exit. Our guide, a young fellow from Oregon State College, made the trip interesting with his explanations and answers to our questions. The fifty cents we each paid for the excursion we deemed money well spent. I had never been in a large cave before and was quite thrilled with the experience. The local chipmunks and we had lunch together before Erce and I started the long downhill ride back to U.S. 199. We made good time until we spied a blackberry patch that detained us until our stomachs were satisfied and we had picked some berries for our next breakfast.

It seems unusual to me now that we came upon so many CCC camps about supper time. We didn't plan it that way because we had no idea where their camps were located. That day I wasn't even particularly hungry when, late in the afternoon, we arrived at a Three-C camp, but that didn't stop me from eating a hearty meal that was offered to me. How could I not do so with all that good food on the table? After a shower, we traveled until almost dark before finding a nice spot to bed-down for the night. The town of Grants Pass lay only a few miles ahead. We had made a better than usual run of sixty-eight miles for the day, but only twenty-eight of that was on the main route.

We spent most of the next day in town waiting for the afternoon mail to arrive. Erce had asked his mother to send him another pair of shoes, but they hadn't come. A little rain fell as we went to a bike shop to buy Rosie some new pedals to replace those broken in the accident. About six we went on to a free campground a few miles north of Grants Pass. I had found an old license plate, so I cut the word, "California," from it and attached it to my bike with the hope that people would stop asking me "where you from?"—but it didn't help much.

In the morning we picked both "breakfast and lunch" from an orchard of peach trees adjacent to our camp. Later in the day we passed many farms and prune orchards. Pickers were being paid five cents a bushel—equal to the cost of one loaf of bread. We picked only a few prunes for our supper and breakfast. We camped just outside of a little "burg" called Myrtle Creek on the bank of the Umpqua River. Erce cooked a delicious meat and vegetable stew for our supper (not from a can). Our run of fifty-six miles for the day was considerably better than the fourteen of the day before.

On August 4th, one month from our start date, we watched with pleasure as my cyclometer turned from 999.9 to 1000.0 miles. We even counted off the last few tenths—"7 . . . 8 . . . 9 . . . one thousand." After passing through Roseburg, we ate lunch and rested in an old pear orchard. In the late afternoon, near the town of Anlauf, we came to a roadside restaurant where we stopped to ask if we could work for some food. The owner gave us each an axe, pointed to the woodpile, and said, "go to work." We split all the blocks into stove-size pieces, but I broke one of the axe handles in the process. I surely hated to have to tell the owner about it, but after doing so he still gave us some good sandwiches to take along. "I am sorry about breaking the handle," I said as I sheepishly took the bag of food.

"Well you split the wood, so we'll call it even," the cook said, rather unhappily I thought.

The dark sky looked like it might rain that night, so when we came to a barn near the road we wheeled our bikes in and looked for a place to sleep. A tractor occupied part of the ground floor, but a loft had some loose hay where we spread out our bedrolls for a sound night's sleep. There wasn't any house around close. I think the owner must have lived in the town of Anlauf just ahead, or in Cottage Grove a few miles beyond.

We had picked some apples and prunes, from one of the many orchards along the way the day before, so had them for our breakfast. The going was easy in the Willamette Valley with level, concrete roads. We crossed the Willamette River and were north of Eugene by lunch time. With a steady tail wind pushing us along we were making about sixteen miles per hour when our second accident occurred. As we passed a fellow standing by his car with its hood up we both looked back at the same time to ask, "Can we help?" That was when we ran together. Although we weren't hurt, Anabelle suffered a broken rim and was unrideable. We got the man's car started for him, but unfortunately for us he took off south bound, without offering to take us to town.

We were about twelve miles south of Albany, and perhaps even near where my farm-family friends lived. We tried thumbing a ride, but didn't have any luck. After juggling our situation around in our minds a bit, we decided to take the packs off Rosie and that I would ride her ahead to try to find my friends, the Briles family. Erce would stay with Anne and the camping gear until I got back, which we hoped wouldn't be very long. Not knowing the Briles' address before we left, I had had no way of letting them know we were coming—so it rested heavily on my mind that even if I did find their farm, still they might not be home. I rode twenty-two miles (checked by car later) and did a lot of inquiring before I finally found the right farm in the late afternoon. It was located east of Albany a few miles in a timbered section of flat land. I saw a woman working in a garden as I approached up a long driveway towards the garden and house.

"Well, Kenny Wise, where did you come from?" I heard the sweet, surprised voice of Gertie (Mrs. Briles) exclaim after she recognized me.

"Oh, just down the road a piece, but I need some help to pick up my traveling companion," I explained.

"Milo is fishing, but should be back with the car soon. Come on in," she welcomed.

I had plenty of time to tell her what happened before Mr. Briles returned. When he did, we went searching for Erce. About ten thirty, after looking in several locations along the road, we finally found him, comfortably asleep under a highway bridge not far from where we had collided several hours before. It was a good thing that Milo had thought to bring a flashlight or else we might not have found him until the next morning.

"Milo, this is Erce—Erce, this is Mr. Briles."

"Howdy, sorry to disturb your sleep."

Erce, Cecil, Gertie, Milo and Ken at Briles Farm in Oregon.

"Quite all right, quite all right," Erce said as he climbed out of his sleeping bag.

We loaded our gear and the broken bike into the back seat of the open touring car and rode back to the farm. Gertie and her children—Cecil, twenty-one, about a year older than me, and Erma, a pretty girl of nineteen—were waiting for us. My family and the Briles had traveled together years ago, so we had a lot of catching up to do—therefore another day had almost arrived before Erce and I made our beds of hay in their barn.

Anne's cyclometer had stopped after traveling sixty-eight miles that day, but Rosie had made ninety miles, a new record of just one half mile more than our first day's ride. The wind on our backs and the flat road had helped, but our stupid accident surely hadn't.

Erce, Cecil, dogs, Ken and big Douglas fir.

Early the next morning Erce rode to town to buy a new rim and tire for Anne, and to check at the post office for our mail. As expected, we didn't have any. He was able to purchase a rim and spokes, but a tire had to be ordered from Portland. We got it a week later from San Francisco—there were no tires for racing-type bikes in the whole state of Oregon. The forced delay of our trip turned out to be a pleasant one.

During the week with the Briles, Erce and I learned much about farm life and farm people. To a couple of city kids everything was new and interesting—even milking cows, which was a kick in more ways than one. Milo and Gertie's seventy-six acre farm, mostly flat land, had been hewn from the forest. Much of it still had large trees on it we discovered when with saws and axes we went to the back forty to make firewood. One two-hundred-year-old Douglas fir we cut down in a few minutes, but then a bigger one gave us a lot of trouble. We made a big undercut the way it should fall, but a wind came up from that direction which made our saw pinch, even though we used wedges. We finally gave up and went swimming in a cold river nearby to wash the sweat off. During the night the wind changed. We heard a distant crash and knew that the big tree had fallen on its own. In the morning we counted annual growth rings. It was a small sapling when the Pilgrims landed at Plymouth Rock. It would have been an excellent saw log for lumber, but we cut it up just for firewood, there being no shortage of timber for lumber mills during the Thirties.

We helped thin raspberry plants, pick beans, and of course weed around the potatoes, corn, and other vegetables in the garden. Gertie, a splendid cook, prepared all that fresh farm produce very well, and how we stowed away her good country-style meals. For poor "city kids" it was a real enjoyable treat. Compared to Three-C camp meals the quantity wasn't any greater, but the quality was much more tasty.

"Milo, does Gertie cook this good for you all the time?" I asked.

"What do you mean, this little meal? You should be here for Thanksgiving—then we have a *good* meal," he proudly said. Milo was a good hunter, and I learned, upon being taken to their cellar, that they had many jars of canned venison as well as vegetables and fruit on their shelves. Home-churned butter, cottage cheese, baked apples, venison, hotcakes, sorghum, and fruit conserves were just a few of the delights on the table. We found that farm folks worked hard, but had a comfortable living. On Saturday night it was their custom for the young people to go to a dance. Erce was a little surprised to learn that farm kids were not much different than their city cousins in their talk, dance, and boy-girl social relations, but perhaps learned them even earlier in life. Trades were learned mainly from their Pas and Mas. Sunday was a day of rest, church, and good times. At one of our leisurely evening talks, Milo told us stories about Eastern Oregon being a cattle country and a wild place to live, somewhat like the Old West.

Finally my bike's new tire came and we got ready to leave the Briles farm after a most interesting and enjoyable week —our only cost being $2.75 for my bike tire, rim, and spokes. We felt sad to leave such jolly good friends and helpful people, but it was time to move on. If we were ever going to get to the Missouri River, we would have to put more miles on our bikes than we had been. It was August 14th and summer was three-fourths spent.

Heading north we soon came to many hop fields with their fifteen foot high trellised vines. Hops, used for brewing, grew well in Oregon because of the abundant rainfall. Near Independence we stopped to ask for a job picking hops, but were told we would have to wait several days for the hops to ripen—so we went on to Salem, the state capital. We had a dusty ride for thirty miles over a rough, rocky road being repaired.

When we got to the Willamette River we took a swim, not far from the capitol building. Some miles north of Salem near a hop field we found a hay stack to use for our camp. Many families were camped near the hop fields waiting for the picking to start. Some of those families traveled from one harvest to another. One fellow told me, "We'll be going to Washington before long to pick apples." With a large family of kids that worked with them they made good money for a short time. From our hay stack bed we watched the moon, a sliver of fire, go down behind green fields. Our run of fifty-five miles made a total of 1,202. We decided not to wait for the hops to fill our pockets with money.

It seemed that only minutes after we watched the moon go down we were looking at a beautiful sunrise from behind a pyramid-shaped Mount Hood with its tip of snow. Bright pink clouds were peeking at sleepy fir trees, and at us as we climbed out of bed early. Soon we were on the road again and crossing the Clackamas River which joins the Willamette. We caught a long truck ride to Portland, arriving in the middle of the afternoon. We went from one barber shop to another until in the sixth one we located Erce's dad. Mr. Hart quit working for the day to take us to his apartment where we cleaned up, had supper, and talked for hours. Erce hadn't seen much of his father since his folks were separated years before, so it was a good reunion for them both.

The next morning the Harts took us riding to St. John and the airport on Swan Island, a large island located in the Willamette River. The rest of the day we spent trying to write a story about our bike trip, to sell to the Portland newspaper. The editors weren't buying, so as journalists we didn't make any money. "We have our own reporters," we were told.

On August 17th we all celebrated Ercell's birthday with a feast and presents. Erce wrote in our log book a story about his coming of age. "Having passed by the Grace of God and my enemies, that magic milestone that marks the completion of twenty-one winters and summers, I can now buy a cow (if I could), marry (if I could), vote (I already do)."

"I'll buy that, even if the newspapers won't," and taking the log book, I finished by writing, "In other words, Ercell had his 21st birthday." I had to put up with his seniority for three more months until the day I also would become a "senior citizen."

The next morning, after getting our free haircuts from Daddy Hart, we left Portland to start the long journey up the Columbia River Gorge. The road followed the river most of the way, but also cut into the mountains in places. What was the main road then, narrow and winding, is now the scenic route traveled only by a few tourists. A freeway along the river now handles the main traffic. We passed through several tunnels cut in the volcanic rock, and saw many beautiful

Ken (left) and Ercell in Portland, Oregon.

waterfalls. The most majestic and famous is called Mult-nomah, and is the main tourist attraction of all the pretty falls.

We knew that the trip from Portland on would be different. We didn't have any more friends or relatives along the way to support us. We were totally on our own. Another important change was our direction of travel from north to east. We were facing the sun in the mornings like the explorers, Lewis and Clark, had done in 1806 on their return trip to Missouri. Yes, we were on the western end of their trail starting up the Columbia River as they had. We didn't know then if we would reach the Missouri River, but we had high hopes of doing so. Really, we had a better chance of success than they did. Lewis and Clark had to travel by canoe on the river, fight Indians who tried to steal from them, and then make a long trip over the mountains along rough trails on horse back. We had fast bikes on good roads and CCC camps and stores to supply our needs. All we had to do was pedal and keep going.

The Columbia is a big river, over a thousand miles long and a mile wide in places. The discoverer, Captain Robert Gray, named it for his ship in 1792. We didn't see any canoes on the river, but we saw a steamer pushing two barges loaded with what we thought might be wheat from the grain growing country of Eastern Washington. When it came time to camp we were just west of Hood River near the place where construction work on the Bonneville Dam was taking place. We found a spot beside the road under some walnut trees to spread our bedrolls. We had made a good day's run of sixty-eight miles—which we thought wasn't too bad for the late start from Portland and the uphill grade all the way, with no pulls by trucks.

In the morning we stopped at the Cascade Falls to watch the water foaming over the rocks. The river, about 1,500 feet wide, had white water tumbling down forty to fifty feet all

Cascades on Columbia River before Bonneville Dam was built.

the way across except at the lock. The Native Americans hold to the story that a natural bridge existed there at one time. We also heard a wild story of how two river stern-wheeler captains were racing down river for the Cascade Locks. The one that was losing, instead of stopping at the locks, went on through the Cascade Falls successfully but later had his captain's papers taken away for doing so. The beautiful falls were covered with water when Bonneville Dam reservoir reached full capacity. We thought it would be our last time to ever see them, and were right.

We passed through the town of Hood River early in the day. The country became more open and semi-desert with sagebrush as we got farther east. The old river had cut through layer upon layer of lava flows, leaving bluffs, abrupt and shelving on both sides on its way to the sea.

We stopped to rest at Celilo Rapids where Native Americans were salmon fishing with dip nets. Some of the rickety platforms hanging from the rock walls, on which the men were balanced, looked like they might fall into the river at any moment. The Indians were skillful with their long handled nets at catching fish trying to make it up the rapids. Their years of experience at the same place had taught them all the tricks they needed to harvest a good supply of salmon. They lived in shacks of all sorts, made of any material they

CELILO FALLS
COLUMBIA RIVER 1934

Natives dipping and drying salmon for winter. The falls have disappeared in the waters of the Dalles Dam. No more is it a "happy hunting grounds."

could salvage, during the fishing season. Some of the women wore moccasins and others had on high-heeled slippers.

The Natives lost their fishing place when the waters of The Dalles Dam covered it forever. Another famous fishing grounds of the Indians was at Kettle Falls on the upper Columbia River near the Canadian border. This twenty-five foot drop was covered with water when the reservoir behind Grand Coulee Dam filled. Again the Natives were defeated. Whatever rights they had were drowned in the name of progress by the white man. We had a swim in a canal beside the river before traveling on.

Ten miles west of Arlington we caught a truck and hung on all the way to town. As the light of day faded away we were still riding, but were getting tired because the weather had been hot all day. Also we had pedaled, or been towed, nearly eighty-five long miles. Beside the road a freight train slowly moved along in the same direction we were going. "Why don't we hitch a ride on that freight?" Erce suggested.

I thought it over about two seconds before answering, "Sure, let's try it." We wheeled our bikes over beside the tracks—then while waiting for a boxcar with an open door to come by, we planned our strategy. Erce said that he would lift the bikes up if I could drag them aboard (sailor talk). We spaced the bikes about a car distance apart, then I walked back along the tracks a little distance to wait.

"Here it comes, get ready," I shouted as I pulled myself up and through the open door of an empty boxcar.

"Grab it, Pee Wee," Erce said as he boosted Anne up and I pulled her on. He then ran forward to do the same for Rosie—with her packs still tied on, front and back. I grabbed her. Then Erce caught up and climbed in.

"All aboard," I said as I took hold of his belt to help him up. Pretty soon the train picked up speed. We were on our way—we knew not where, but we were going in the right direction anyway.

By that time the sun had just set behind the hills skirting the Columbia River valley. We sat in the doorway eating raisin sandwiches while watching "the country move by." Our food supply at the time was a bit low because we didn't want to carry any extra weight on those hot days and on the uphill climb. Before long darkness had consumed all, so we rolled out our beds on the hard floor to get some rest. The rhythm of the wheels on the tracks, clicking at every rail joint, soon made us sleepy. I thought as I drifted off to sleep that being a railroad bum wasn't so bad. The tracks followed the river and we had seen other people riding in boxcar doorways, and sometimes on top of a car—so why not us? It was a much used mode of transportation for hobos during the Depression. The trainmen, "Bulls," seldom "kicked" anyone off an empty freight train.

4

Washington—Idaho—
Montana

The sun shone into the boxcar door and all was quiet as we awakened. We had been side-tracked. I could see a town nearby, but couldn't see the highway. We located it as a car went by about a hundred yards away with two fences between it and us. After some struggling getting our bikes over these obstacles, we were back on the road again, riding into Umatilla. The small town had only a few stores and a railroad station. The train had carried us forty-six miles during the night. We were hungry, so found a grocery store to stock up on food—which included four cantaloupes, some watermelon, and a quart of milk all for ten cents. We ate half of this just outside the store.

The Columbia River and the highway had turned north. The bluffs on the banks were not so high as before.

Early in the day we rolled into the Evergreen State of Washington. "Evergreen State?" It was a desert. We couldn't see a tree—nothing but rocks and sagebrush. Finally we got to Pasco. It felt like it might have been over 100° so we rested for a few hours in a shady park. We decided it was too hot to ride. Later, after it had cooled down some, we went eighteen miles farther and camped by a pond of water in a pothole beside the road.

We had crossed the Snake River, the Columbia's largest tributary, just a few miles before getting to Pasco. At that point we left the Lewis and Clark Trail. They had come down the Snake River in 1805 and continued on down the Columbia River to the Pacific Ocean, returning in 1806 by the same route. We would join their trail again at the Missouri River, but for awhile we would be on just the "Hart—Wise Trail."

From Pasco we headed northeast, away from the river, toward Spokane. Even though we had taken it easy most of the day, we had added another sixty-two miles to our journey. We burned sage for our campfire that night.

All the sagebrush around us reminded me of my trapping trip on the Mojave Desert in California my first winter out of high school. A friend of the family, about my Dad's age, stopped by in his home-made camper. He told us he was going trapping and wanted to know if Dad could go with him. Dad had a rare job at the time so suggested that he might want to take me along. Mr. Spainhower looked me over for awhile before saying, "Okay you can go if you want to, but remember we'll be gone all winter." It was mid-October at the time.

I didn't have anything else to do and thought it would be neat to travel and trap—something I had never done—so I readily said, "I'll go." I got my clothes, boots, Kodak, and an old .22 rifle together and the next morning after breakfast Spainhower and I started north. He had a one-ton flatbed

Boulder Canyon and dam site where a platform filled with men
broke, dropping them to their deaths on the rock,
700 feet below.

truck onto which he had build a camper. It looked half like a sheepherder's wagon with a small wood-burning stove inside. The stovepipe stuck through the metal roof like a flag pole. The other half looked like a modern pickup camper with a bed extension built over the truck cab. This could have been the very first of its kind.

We went north as far as Ely, Nevada without ever setting a trap, then drifted south through the sagebrush country. Wherever we found signs of coyotes we would stop a few days to set traps. Not catching any we would go on to a different location and try again.

We got east as far as the southwest tip of Colorado where one day we stopped at Four States Corners, not far from Mesa Verde National Park. There I had the thrill of putting one hand on the ground of Utah, another in Colorado while one foot was placed in Arizona and the other in New Mexico. I looked like a turtle in doing the feat that could be done nowhere else in any of the other states.

From there we traveled across Arizona to the south tip of Nevada. We passed through Las Vegas—a small place then—and stopped at Boulder Canyon south of there where a dam was being constructed to hold back the water of the Colorado River. At the time, 1932, it was called Boulder Dam but later changed to Hoover Dam in Black Canyon. I remember being told about an accident which had happened shortly before our arrival. Cables stretched across the canyon supported a platform that rode on pulleys out to the middle of the canyon and then lowered to the work site at the bottom. Workmen rode the platform up and down every day. The accident occurred when a cable broke, dumping a load of workers to their death on the rocks hundreds of feet below.

The dam was to be 727 feet high and would create the largest man-made lake in the world. Lake Mead, formed by the dam, is now a favorite recreational play area of skiers and boaters. Also, when finished it would bring irrigation waters to the desert, making Imperial Valley of California one of the richest garden producing areas in the United States, besides supplying hydroelectric power to Los Angeles and other cities. Seeing that marvelous undertaking made the trip really worthwhile for me.

We finally ended up on the Mojave Desert in an area between Barstow and Victorville where we set up camp to do some serious trapping. There Spainhower caught our first coyote. He had taught me how to set the number three traps, cover and bait them, wipe out my foot tracks and put some stinky scent around, all for nought. I never caught anything except a few jack rabbits, and most of them the coyotes fed on before I got back to the trap. Once a cougar circled one of my sets, but it never touched the bait, nor did I get to see it— just its tracks.

The funniest thing happened one day when Spainhower's little Mexican Chihuahua, (smallest of all dog

Spainhower beside his home-made camper—1932.

breeds) with its sweater on, spotted a jack rabbit and took off after it. The jack, about three times bigger than the dog, would take a few hops and wait for it to catch up. Then the rabbit jumped sideways behind some brush and watched the Chihuahua dash on by, and even hopped after it a little way, seeming quite curious as to what kind of an animal had chased him. It took us almost an hour to find the pooped-out dog that had lost the jack and itself by running on in a straight line until it could run no more.

Although I had a good time with Spainhower, I was beginning to get—kid fashion—a bit discouraged and homesick. A few days before Christmas I told my good companion, "I want to go home."

"You're welcome to go, but I'm not taking you," he said. I think we were getting a little tired of each other's company at that time. As we were not very far from a main road, I took my coat and a few things to eat and started walking. Soon I hitched a ride and made it home in a couple days, never to try trapping again. Some of the area where we trapped in the Mojave is now covered with housing developments.

Early the next morning we met a Japanese farmer loading his truck with garden produce for market. He gave us six small cantaloupes, and we ate four of them for breakfast. The weather was still hot, but getting a tow for fifteen miles out of Connell helped cool us some. Two kids from Frisco were hitching a ride in the same truck. They traveled faster than we did by getting rides all the way. Before getting to the town of Lind we came upon a water trough, that the cattle had temporarily abandoned. It was brim full of cool water, so we shed our shorts and had a refreshing bath. The shady trees and cool grass in the park at Lind relieved us from the sun as we flopped on the lawn for awhile. When some clouds took the glare out of the sun's force, we rode on until almost dark.

One and a half miles beyond Ritzville we found a place to camp at an abandoned gun club. Unpacking our gear disclosed the fact that we were out of water and there wasn't any there.

"Flip you to see who goes to get water, Pee Wee."

"Okay, you have a coin?"

"Call it."

"Tails," I said.

"Heads it is. Get on your bike," Erce commanded, smiling. Having lost, I rode back to town to fill our canteens. By the time I got back my cyclometer registered 71 miles for the day.

August 22nd found us trying to catch trucks going to Spokane. They were all going too fast so we had to make it on our own pedal-power. As we neared the small city, ponderosa pine became increasingly more numerous. We were glad to see trees again. In the distance loomed the Bitterroot Mountains of Idaho where we were heading. When we got to the Post Office Erce went in while I stayed with our bikes. He came out shaking his head, which I knew meant we had no mail. Although we liked to get mail, we didn't expect it at every place. Erce had received his newer shoes at Albany while we were on the farm, and none too soon, because his old ones were falling apart.

We rented a room at the YMCA, mainly to have a good hot shower. Erce wrote a story about our trip and tried to sell it to the newspaper editor, but he wouldn't buy it. We figured the failure was because of an American Legion convention in town that took all the newspaper space. We hadn't yet come to realize that newspaper people don't buy stories like we were trying to sell. We weren't interested in notoriety, just trying to earn some money. "Better luck next time," I said sympathetically.

"I must have the wrong approach, because I have heard

about other travelers selling their stories," Erce commented.

"But maybe not to newspapers," I suggested.

The Legionnaires were parading down the street in their pajamas early the next morning as we left Spokane on U.S. 10 toward Idaho. By lunch time we had reached the beautiful Lake Coeur d'Alene in Idaho—the Gem State.

K Wise — Lake Coeur d'Alene

This large lake, 24 miles long with 125 miles of shore line, has been rated as one of the five most beautiful lakes in the world. Maybe that was by the local Chamber of Commerce, I don't know, but along with Pend Oreille and Priest Lakes, a little farther north, I would rate all three as very high on my list of beauty spots. In the early days many steamboats plied the waters of Lake Coeur d'Alene hauling miners, lumbermen, and their supplies to the head of the lake and up the rivers. The steamboat era ended when the railroads were built and started hauling freight. Probably the last boat, the *Flyer* owned by Potlatch Forest Timber Company, was still making trips up the lake to St. Maries on the "Shadowy St. Joe River" in 1934. In 1938 she was deliberately burned as "being of no further use," the owners stated. Today an excursion boat makes Sunday trips on the lake during the summer months. Later in my life I married a lovely Idaho girl and spent most of my life living in beautiful Idaho.

Lake Coeur d'Alene in northern Idaho.

We had a swim in the lake's cold waters just east of the town of Coeur d'Alene before traveling on toward Montana. The Idaho Panhandle that we were crossing is only about seventy-five miles wide. We were passing through white pine and red cedar forests on an uphill gravel road, so we did some walking. Near the top of the grade a truck came along and we hooked on—later we even used it for a brake going down the other side. We had supper at a highway workers' camp. Man! The food was good—and free, too. Our own camp meals were not too varied, so when we chanced to have a meal prepared by a professional cook, we relished the occasion. What a difference in the temperature from just a day before—after sundown the air was downright cold. We found a couple of haystacks and made our bed between them for some protection from the weather. The full moon rose, screened by smoke from a nearby forest fire, looking blood red. As we lay in bed thinking about our sixty mile ride from Spokane, the moon slowly sailed away behind some tall pine trees.

On the following day we passed through Kellogg, a town almost totally sustained by the mining industry located nearby. There were smelters and mine openings with tailings along some hillsides. We learned that silver and lead were the main ores being found in the area.

We caught a slow truck just outside of town that towed us ten miles—all the way to Wallace, another mining town. We rode on for seven miles to a small place called Mullan. It had been named after Captain John Mullan, who engineered and directed the building of the military wagon road from Fort Walla Walla, Washington to Fort Benton, Montana in 1859 to 1862. This Mullan Trail, one of the most important wagon roads in the Pacific Northwest, opened up the territory to mining and settlement. The Indians told Mullan he could never get through the Idaho mountains, but the young lieutenant had only shrugged. With a crew of about a hun-

Clark Fork River in Montana.

dred and fifty men, Mullan did the "impossible." When the 624-mile road was completed, troops and supplies could be transported from the head of navigation of the Missouri River to Walla Walla and beyond. Years later the Mullan Trail also provided a route over the Bitterroot Mountains for two bums on bikes.

Standing at a gas station at the edge of town, Erce and I knew that because of the increased grade and gravel road, we would have to walk all the way to the summit if we started on. Therefore we waited for a truck to come along. When an empty one came into the service station, we asked for a ride. The driver was willing, so we lifted our bikes on and rode with him over fifty miles—all the way to Superior, Montana, the Treasure State. We traveled up to almost 5,000 feet in elevation before starting down the Montana side. The country was timbered, with some cutover areas with new growth starting. The road followed beside the lively St. Regis River most of the way.

It joined the Clark Fork, a larger river, at the town of St. Regis. We were now in what Montana people call "the Big Sky Country," for its openness. The mountains had spread leaving a big flat valley where some cattle roamed. The name was fitting, I thought. We thanked the truck driver for the ride, then rode on a few miles to camp beside the Clark Fork, named for William Clark of the Lewis and Clark Expedition. We had traveled over one hundred miles, but pedaled only forty-two of it.

The next morning we awoke just in time to see "our" truck go by, on the highway. We rode along beside the river until noon, then had a swim in it to wash the road dust off us before having lunch. Our frequent swims, during the warm weather, helped to keep us clean during the bike trip. Shortly after lunch a young fellow in a delivery truck gave us a nineteen-mile ride into Missoula, a large town and headquarters for Region I of the U.S. Forest Service. Erce had lived in Missoula for awhile when very young.

"I can't remember a thing about this place," Erce joked. There were many railroad bums at the yards waiting for trains, which was an indication that there weren't many jobs being offered. Still there were men at the Forestry Department Office inquiring about forest firefighting work. We thought about trying to get employment, but decided that because summer was about over we had better be getting along to the Missouri River. We went on through town to open country to find a spot to camp. Locating a convenient place between a hay stack and a corn field, we pulled over, leaned our bikes against the stack, and proceeded to make our camp. We didn't see a farm house and the corn looked ripe and tempting, so we picked a few ears to go with our rice and pudding for supper. It was a good meal, and we even thought we might take some corn with us the next day.

A farmer awakened us in the morning with his pitchfork. "What are you doing here?" he asked gruffly.

"Just traveling through," I told him. "You better be on your way then," he strongly suggested. Although I am sure he saw our stolen corn husks from the night before, he didn't say anything about them. We made haste to leave and at the same time tried to excuse our presence there and thank him all at once. He didn't say anything more, but just stood there watching until we were out of his sight. I am sure he didn't like bums having a fire so close to his hay stack—and I couldn't blame him. Needless to say, we didn't get any corn to take along.

The next day, Sunday August 26th, we rode about fifteen miles to where we found an abandoned farm. We stopped to pick some apples after first making sure there were no farmers with pitchforks around. In the afternoon near the town of Clinton, we tried to get on a freight train, but were too far from the tracks when it started. A couple of fences and an irrigation ditch slowed us down or we would have made it.

Later we stopped at a farm and bought two quarts of milk, some bread, and were given two hot cinnamon rolls. After making fifty-seven miles, we spotted an isolated hay stack where we hoped that we wouldn't be disturbed for the night, and rolled our bikes over to it. A ladder lay nearby, so we leaned it against the stack to climb up and make our beds right in the middle on top. The nights had gotten increasingly colder, but we slept warm that night with a big mattress under us. A large, bright moon coasted along above us as we thought about many things, but mainly of nearing the end of our bike trip, and could we trade Annabelle and Rosie for a canoe to float the Missouri River? "How much farther to the river?" I asked Erce because I had seen him looking at our Montana road map earlier.

"Oh, about seventy-five miles, but then we have another fifty to Great Falls. We have to get beyond there, unless you want to go over the falls in a canoe."

"No, thanks. How much are you going to ask for Rosie?"

"Maybe twelve or fifteen dollars."

"I'll ask more for my Anne because she's prettier."

"Go to sleep, Pee Wee."

We were a little late getting out of our cozy bed in the morning, but once on the road the pedaling warmed us. Going into the foothills of the Rocky Mountains we came to a section of freshly oiled road. Our bike tires picked up the oil and threw it all over our bikes and clothes. What a mess and a time we had cleaning up.

Later we came up to a car that had a flat tire. The owner didn't have a jack, so Erce rode back to a farm where he borrowed one and we changed a tire for the old fellow. He promised to pay us fifty cents at his bakery when we got to Helena where he said he lived. I returned the jack. At noon we stopped at a farm and had a lunch of raw cabbage, carrots, and cauliflower for ten cents. We were wearing only our Scout shorts. The farm people stared at us and called us nudists. Maybe we looked like Indians, too—because of our bronzed skin caused by many days spent riding bareback in the sunshine. We used olive oil to protect our skin from burning.

We came to a place on the road toward Helena where we couldn't ride because the surface was soft dirt, so we were walking along when we met a fellow loading firewood, he had cut, into his truck. We loaded it for him and he gave us a ride to Helena, the state capital. On the way we climbed over the Continental Divide on McDonald Pass at an elevation of 6,500 feet. From that point the drainage was eastward toward the Missouri River, and we would be on a downhill grade to it—we thought.

We had crossed the Rocky Mountains, which at that point wasn't very rocky or seemed high either, because all the surrounding country was relatively high also. Helena became "Queen City of the West" when gold was discovered in that area in 1864. Her main street, Last Chance Gulch, has historic buildings dating back to the 1870s.

In town we found the bakery where we collected the fifty cents owed us for changing the tire. The owner also gave us a loaf of bread and two cakes, and at an ice cream parlor we bought a pint of vanilla to go with our cake which we ate there. We had a delicious dessert before our supper, but also spent half of our hard earned money.

On our way to the "Y" we stopped at a little cafe for something more to eat. As we started to enter two men pushed us aside as they came out, got into their car, and hurriedly drove off. Once inside the diner we could tell that something was wrong because the owner and a waitress were carrying on a loud conversation. We learned that the two fellows had shortchanged the girl out of five bucks. They were on their way by the time she discovered it. We felt sorry for her but were a bit late to help.

By the time we had finished taking our free showers at the YMCA it had turned fairly dark outside. We rode out of town anyway to find a place to camp because our finances were pretty low. We were lucky to soon find a hay stack—really a bean stack, but about as comfortable as hay—where we stopped to sleep for the night. We were close to the road, but not many cars traveled it at night so we slept well.

The next day we rode and walked up and over a small mountain range from which we had our first view of the Missouri River and the "Gates of the Mountains." Although we were seeing them from the back side it was still an impressive view for me just to see the big river. The Gates, discovered and named by Lewis and Clark July 19, 1805, are sheer cliffs rising 1,200 feet above the river on both sides. The country on the down river side is low in comparison to the mountainous terrain above the Gates, thus I thought the name was appropriate.

We were thrilled to be back on the Lewis and Clark Trail again and to "rediscover the Gates," August 28, 1934. We rode north through a hot valley and down a canyon to Wolf Creek. Three miles farther on we crossed the Missouri River —the first time ever for me. I didn't expect it to be so large, over a hundred yards wide, and fast moving. We decided that it would be fun for us to ride the river in a canoe and we were anxious to do so.

Rosie had two flat tires, so Erce walked. We stopped at a service station to inflate Rosie's tires and for a drink of water. A big man from Georgia (we assumed he was from there by his car license) struck up a conversation with us by asking the usual question, "Where you fellows from?"

"California."

"Ride those bikes all the way?"

"Most of it," I said, showing him Anne's cyclometer that registered 1,880 miles. He then bought us some pop to drink. After some more talk he got us each an ice cream cone. Most of our conversations weren't that profitable—we had answered those same questions seemingly hundreds of times for nothing—and when people had asked those, they usually went on to ask, "Don't you ever get tired?", "How long have you been on the road?", "How many miles do you make a day?", and of course "Where are you going?"

We stopped in back of a farm on a small creek to wash our clothes. The owner of the farm had been watching us set up camp and shortly afterward came to see us, bringing eighteen ears of corn and a quart of milk for our supper. Later, two boys who worked at the farm brought us some cabbage, carrots, and cucumbers, then sat around the fire to talk with us for awhile. We had an excellent supper and enjoyed the

Anabelle and Rosie — E. Hart on 2000 Mile Bike trip-1934.

company. Most people were very interested in our trip and
really good to us all along the way. Our run that day equaled
forty-four miles.

It sprinkled a little that night and was cloudy in the
morning, so our washing hadn't dried. Ercell went fishing
and actually came back with a trout which I cooked for
lunch. I wrote the log book up to date. About 4:30, with
clean clothes, we rode on, but Rosie's rear tire, leaking air
like it had run over a porcupine, was about flat again.

A fisherman by the road loaned us the use of a pump
from his car. He and his wife and another couple were eating
a picnic supper and they invited us to partake with them, so
we graciously "partook." They were very friendly, jolly people, and we had fun talking to them while filling our stom-

achs. On our wheels again we made a few miles before a cloud opened up and it began to sprinkle. The day was about over anyway, so when we saw a farmhouse, it looked inviting and we headed down the driveway towards it. Coming up to a man near the house, I asked, "Would you have a shelter where we could spend the night?"

"Sure, there's a bunkhouse around back where you can stay."

"Thanks a lot, mister. It would be wet outdoors for us tonight."

"Where you from" was his first question, and once again we went through our familiar "question—answer game."

The bunkhouse had some old army cots on which we spread our bedrolls. As I sat on the bed reading a magazine, a parade of bedbugs and fleas began. We squished all in sight, then slid into bed with foreboding, expecting a lousy night. Our run for the day had been only twenty-one miles— one of those take-it-easy days of which we didn't have very many. The next morning we were delightfully awakened by a breakfast bell. We hurriedly dressed, having high hopes of being invited to eat. We weren't disappointed. The farmer asked us in the house to a hot, tasty meal, which of course we couldn't turn down.

The weather had turned a bit gusty and cold as we pedaled along beside the Missouri River most of the day. The hills were barren of trees, but had good grass and we often saw cattle grazing. We passed places along the river shore where cottonwoods, with shiny heart-shaped leaves waving in the wind, grew tall. We stopped in the shelter of some to eat lunch and wash our feet in the muddy Missouri. We decided it was too dirty for swimming.

We passed through the town of Cascade—I think there must be a town with that name on every river. About thirty miles farther we topped a hill and could see ahead—Great Falls, the objective of our 2,000 mile bike journey. Just before getting to town we crossed the Sun River near where it runs into the Missouri, making Old Muddy, as it is called, even muddier and some wider. We wondered if we would get to see it grow wider later on as we paddled a canoe down its winding course.

In town we looked for the Boy Scout executive, hoping he might give us some leads on where we could find a place to stay and possibly know of a canoe for sale. At his home Mrs. Ralph Cook, his wife, invited us in and told us her husband was away at Scout Camp winding things up for the season but would be home in a day or two. I told her about our plans, how we intended to sell our bikes, buy a canoe, and voyage down the Missouri to St. Louis. She kindly told us we were welcome to stay in her basement until we could do so. She was a brave and generous young lady. I believe a woman would be unwise to do a thing like that today. Although we were half-way clean, we were total strangers to her. She provided us with some camp cots to sleep on. We brought our bags in and left them there while we rode downtown to see if we could sell our bikes. At a bicycle shop the owner said, "I could never sell them."

"Why not?" I asked. "They are good racing bikes."

"That's just the trouble. Kids around here want the new balloon-tired bikes which work better on our gravel roads."

He was right. Our narrow tires were not much good except on paved roads. In the Thirties the balloon tire was even bigger around than the tire a mountain bike uses today. We still had hopes of selling our bikes, so we put signs on them—Anne, $15.00, and Rosie, $12.00—and rode around town. People stared at us, and we even heard a few comments like "look at the old-fashioned bicycles," or "narrow seats." We inquired about other Scout leaders and met a Mr. McCoy, President of the Boy Scout Council. He gave us a couple of leads on canoes, which upon inquiring we learned were not for sale. We went back to the Cook's place a little discouraged but still determined.

The last day of August had arrived. We had talked to the editor of the *Great Falls Tribune* the day before. He wrote a very nice story about our trip and we received some free advertising about our desire to sell our bikes and buy a canoe. When this came out in the paper, we thought it might help but as the days slipped by we found that it didn't. We even placed an ad in the paper, but that didn't help either. We could find no one interested in buying our bikes and no one wanted to sell a canoe because of the coming duck hunting season, when they would be used. It seemed there were many duck hunters in the area.

Mr. Cook arrived home on September 1st and we had a good talk about Scouting and Scout Camps. He didn't seem at all concerned that we were camping in his basement—in fact he had some candy and food supplies left from camp and told us to use whatever we wanted from them. We celebrated Labor Day with the townspeople at the Fairgrounds, saw a parade, and voted for a County Fair Queen.

Someone offered Erce $3.50 for Rosie, which he turned down. After that we realized we weren't going to be able to sell our bikes for what we wanted, and the prospect of getting a canoe was nil. Our hopes for a river canoe trip were about gone and our disappointment showed on our faces. It was then that Ralph Cook offered an alternative. "You might get passes on a stock train going to Chicago," he suggested.

"How do we do that?" Erce quickly asked.

"You find a rancher shipping cattle who isn't going to use his passes."

"That sounds like a good idea," I said, getting interested right away. "Maybe we could get to the World's Fair that way."

Ralph told us that a rancher who shipped cattle east would receive one or two passes, from the railroad, to the destination of the cattle—be it St. Paul, Chicago, New York, or other places. The owner could go himself, which he seldom did, or send someone else—usually he sent one or two of his hands to keep tabs on the cattle. Ercell and I talked about Mr. Cook's suggestion that night, and decided we should shift our efforts in that direction the next day.

On September 4th, two months after leaving Santa Monica, we rode Anne and Rosie to the freight office. While Erce hitched a ride to Cascade to check on cattle shippers, I prepared and shipped our bikes home. I noted the mileage on my cyclometer before saying goodbye to our good steeds —it was 2,010 miles. The shipping cost reduced our finances by $4.43. To help make up for some of this, I went to the deserted fairgrounds and picked up empty beer bottles to turn in at the store for the deposit on them—making sixty cents for my efforts. I had seen the bottles being discarded the day before.

The next day we again went looking for a rancher who would give us his passes in exchange for us taking care of his cattle shipped on the train. Great Falls and towns near there were all shipping points, and possibilities for us to meet ranchers. We rode to Belt with Ralph, then walked to Armington. Not finding a shipper in either place, Erce went to Stanford while I hitched a ride back to Great Falls to help Mr. Cook unload a truck filled with coal that he had bought for his home furnace.

September 7th we hitched a ride to Craig where cattle were being loaded. A rancher there offered us one pass, but didn't have two, so we turned it down. We rode the stock train back to Great Falls, where I learned we could have had two passes if we had gone to Wolf Creek instead of Craig. That was a disappointment for us.

The next day we received a promising lead from Mr. Leavitt, a Boy Scout Commissioner, and who also worked for the Great Northern Railroad Company. He told us the

Long—Clary Stock Company was shipping the next Tuesday and we might get passes from them. We found and talked to Mr. Clary. He was encouraging and told us "I'll let you know by Monday."

Sunday, with nothing much to do, we spent some time at the YMCA, then tried to break the dreariness of waiting by taking a hike along the Missouri River. We were glad we had because we got to see the world's largest fresh water spring at what is now Giant Springs State Park. The clear water rushing from the rocks showed quite a contrast to the muddy water of the river.

While in Great Falls we probably passed by Charles M. Russell's art studio many times, but we didn't know about the talented cowboy artist at that time. Years later I did visit the little log cabin where Russell created his great horse and cowboy oil paintings. We finished the day by washing our weather-beaten clothes.

On Monday Mr. Clary phoned and said, "We'll give you passes, be ready to leave in the morning." We would have several carloads of Long—Clary cattle to take care of. The passes might be to St. Paul, Minnesota or, if the cattle were not sold there, to Chicago, Illinois. When Ercell hung up the receiver, he had a big smile on his face and when he shared the good news, I did too. We were elated with the news and the prospect of traveling again. Also we had been at the Cook's place for eleven nights and felt we really had over-extended our welcome. They were very nice to us and didn't seem to mind that we used their basement all that time. The Cooks lived by a Boy Scout law—"A Scout is a friend to all and a brother to every other Scout."

We were up early on Tuesday, September 11th, packed our things, thanked Mr. and Mrs. Cook for their kindness and bid them goodbye, then hurriedly walked to the stock-yards and train. The cars were still being loaded. We were about three hours early, but that didn't matter as we didn't have anything else to do except buy some food which we had already done earlier. A stock train doesn't carry a dining car —not even for the cattle.

At the train office we were given the long-sought-for passes and a fellow showed us which cattle cars were ours to watch over on the trip. We wrote down the car numbers— otherwise we couldn't have told one car from another. Our only chore was to see that the cattle had water to drink and to keep them on their feet. If a steer got down he might be trampled by the other cattle. We had a long pole to poke any critter wanting to take it easy. Actually the train crew did most of the work, we just had to make sure it was done.

A coach car was provided for our riding comfort. It had seats with backs that lowered to make a bed, but there were no curtains. When we finally got going we realized that many cars made up the train, and there were quite a few men in the coach besides us. Some were owners, but most were cowboys who worked for the outfit they represented. After the round-up they were off to have a good time, and a good time they had, joking and talking about their riding and roping. Many had brought cases of beer along, and we hadn't traveled many miles before a couple of poker games had been started. We were invited to play, but excused ourselves by saying, "We don't have any money"—which was almost true. I didn't know how to play poker and would have lost had I tried it.

The train followed the course of the Missouri River to Fort Benton where Erce and I would have started our canoe trip had that been our destiny. Although we had dreamed about a canoe trip almost from the beginning of our bike ride, as we rode along on the train we started to think that events had worked out for the best after all. A canoe trip down the Missouri would have taken us at least two months, time we couldn't spare—we rationalized—if we were going to Chicago to see the World's Fair. It would close at the end of October, which meant that if we had gone by canoe we would have missed the Fair. As we had no choice, the Fair became more important to us. My canoe trip down the Missouri River had to wait, but the long-dreamed-of trip did finally come to be.

Forty-four years later, my wife Marian and I canoed from Fort Benton down the river, one hundred and fifty miles, through the newly established Upper Missouri National Wild and Scenic River area. It is an area called the Missouri Breaks because of the many odd shaped hills, cliffs, pinnacles with flat rock caps at their tops, and washes. One narrow ridge has a hole through it, and is known as the Hole In The Wall. The Montana Fish and Game Commission has established a Missouri River Recreation Waterway Site there. There are white cliffs, black ones, and ever changing scenes as the river flows along beside them.

A few not-too-scary rapids makes the canoeing interesting but not difficult. It is an area rich in historical events. First to come were Lewis and Clark, followed by the mountain men. Forts were built and steamboats came all the way to Fort Benton. We stopped at the mouth of the Maria's River where Lewis and Clark camped for ten days in order to decide which fork was the true Missouri. They left a cache of food there to be picked up on their return trip. We took five leisurely days to make the enjoyable trip, camping at night on cottonwood flats. We had with us a map showing the course of the river and points of interest like the location of places where Lewis and Clark had camped on their Voyage of Discovery. They would be amazed if they could see today's speedboats racing up the river that they struggled to ascend in their pirogues. We weren't amazed, just disgusted at the noise and disturbance they caused us, as we tried to imagine ourselves back in former years canoeing with Lewis and Clark.

As the train rolled along and the poker game continued, Erce and I made a bed on the seats and slept without covers in the warm coach. We rode through the cold, rainy night and awakened in the morning surprised that we were still in Montana—a big state, with lots of cattle country in the eastern part. At Havre more cattle cars and another coach were added to the train. Eastern Montana looked dry and we didn't see many trees. When we got to North Dakota the country appeared even drier. From my limited view I didn't see anything that would attract me to live there.

The train stopped at Minot where the cattle were fed and watered. Erce and I checked on "our" cattle and all were being cared for without trouble. We watched the loading of both sheep and cattle from the pens alongside the tracks. The train didn't get moving again until late afternoon. It took a long time to unload the cattle, feed them, clean the cars, then reload. Once we were rolling again the poker game started immediately and continued both day and night. Sometimes a cowboy would leave the game long enough to come talk to us. We learned much about life on the range from them.

Friday we awakened somewhere in Minnesota and enjoyed looking out the window at the pretty green country with many lakes. It appeared more to my liking than what we had passed through the day before in North Dakota. The train stopped at the stockyards in South St. Paul about four-thirty in the afternoon. We had been riding through the big city for some time before getting there. It was the largest place we had seen since leaving Portland, Oregon.

We handed in our passes and a letter we had from the Long–Clary Stock Company of Great Falls at the office, then we waited around while the letter was read. After awhile a man came over to us, handed us some new passes, saying "That should fix you boys up. Continue on the same train." We were jubilant, because we didn't know what we would have done had we not gotten the passes. Evidently our friends in Great Falls had put in a good word for us, because the passes we got were not for the Long–Clary cattle.

We had a few hours to look around and get some more food to eat on the way. We had about cleaned out our lunch sack on the four day trip from Great Falls. I got to see the big Mississippi River for the first time in my life. It looked big to me even though it had come only 527 miles from its source on a 1,300 mile journey to the sea. About ten the train was made up and we left St. Paul. Some of the cowboys were gone, but there were a few newcomers—including four dark skinned Native Americans—in the coach with us. We didn't get to talk to them much because they kept to themselves. Before Erce and I turned in for the night we looked at our passes. One was to Roselawn, Indiana and the other one to Brooklyn, New York.

"Well, which one do you want, Pee Wee?"

"I'll flip you, Ex-Pard."

1 have no idea now why we kept such a detailed account of our expenses during the bike trip, but I am glad that we did. It is interesting to look back to see what we ate and how little it cost us to live compared to today's prices. Imagine buying three pounds of raisins for just eighteen cents, or getting a hair cut for only fifteen cents. The fifty-seven days that it took us to get to Great Falls cost $15.58 or 27⅓ cents per day. Food cost us $6.90 and other items $8.68. Of course we did a lot of bumming during those days, otherwise we would never have made it as far as we did on the money we had when we started.

I have copied our expense account just as it was put down in our log book. If you want to know what food and some other things cost back in 1934, have a peep and be surprised at the Bum's account listed here.

BUM'S ACCOUNT

July		
4	Bread	.08
5	Milk	.10
6	Bananas	.08
7	Raisins & Plums	.16
	Room at "Y"	.76
	Olive Oil & Bakery	.20
9	Neverleak	.25
10	Boat Fares - S.F.	.70
11	Watermelon	.12
	Neverleak	.25
12	Bread & Steak	.25
13	Raisins	.10
14	Milk, Meat, Raisins	.34
15	Cheese, Rice, Butter	
	& Raisins	.28
	Vulcanize Patch	.25
	Tape	.10
	Neverleak	.25
28	Milk	.07
	Raisins	.10
30	State Tax	.01
	Post Cards	.02
	Bread	.05
	Meat & Cheese	.20
	2 lbs. Figs, dried	.20
	Candy	.04
	Spokes	.10
31	Milk	.10
	Hamburger	.10

August		
1	Raisins - 2 lbs.	.15
	Trip through Caves	1.00
	Pedals for Rosie	1.00

2	Hamburger, B. & B.	.30
	Rice	.07
	Oatmeal	.10
3	Meat	.15
	Vegetables	.05
4	Cheese	.10
	Bread	.10
	Sugar	.10
	Raisins - 2 lbs.	.17
6	Spokes & Rim	1.00
	Postcard	.01
13	Tire	1.75
	Glue	.15
	Postage for Shoes	.28
14	Postage	.02
	Bread	.07
15	Comb	.05
	Cheese - 1 lb.	.20
	Raisins - 3 lbs.	.19
	Nucoa	.10
17	Tape	.07
	Spoke	.02
20	4 cants, 1 qt. milk	.10
	Meat	.20
	Raisins - 3 lbs.	.18
	Bread	.08
	2 Spokes	.05
22	Bread	.09
	Cheese	.12
	Ice Cream	.15
	Cake	.15
	Tomatoes	.05
	Room at "Y"	.50
23	Milk	.09
	Donuts	.10
	Raisins	.29

	Bread	.06		Freight on bikes	4.43
	Bologna	.10		Postage	.09
24	Cheese	.12	5	Candy	.05
	Milk	.09		Milk	.10
25	Apples	.05	7	Raisins	.33
26	2 qts. milk	.10		Apples	.02
27	Pt. of Ice Cream	.25	8	Hamburger	.05
	Soup, veg., 2 bowls	.20		Beets	.10
	2 cakes & bread	.00		Milk	.30
			10	Bread	.10

57 days to Great Falls   *15.58*

30	Tape & gas	.16	11	Raisins	.30
	Pork & beans	.15		Bologna	.10
	Bread	.05	12	2 cans of fish	.25
	Oatmeal	.10		Milk	.10
	Bologna	.10		Bread	.13
31	Raisins & postage	.40	13	Bananas	.16
	Milk	.20		Bread (moldy)	.10
	Neverleak	.15		Bologna	.15
	Postcard	.01	14	Postage	.10
	1½ lbs. hamburger	.15		Bread	.10
	Bread	.05		Salmon	.13
	News adv. - Canoe	.10			

74 days to Chicago   *26.02*

September

1	Postage	.06	15	Room at "Y"	?
	Peanut butter - 2 lbs.	.25	16	Milk	.10
	Tomatoes	.23		Bought lunch	.40
	Cheese	.17	17	Streetcar fare	.14
	Rice - 4 lbs.	.25		Ticket to fair	2.00
	Salt - 2 lbs.	.07		Donuts	.05
	Milk	.10		Chili at fair	.20
2	Milk	.10		Supper	.25
3	Bread	.10		Room	.25
	Milk	.10	18	Candy (total)	.40
4	Hamburger	.10		Breakfast	.30
	Milk	.10		Supper	.35
				Postage	.10
				Room	.25

19	Uniform	5.00	Development	.40
	Streetcar fare	.14	Total for pictures	2.81
	Breakfast & lunch	.42		
	Bananas	.10		

19	Uniform	5.00
	Streetcar fare	.14
	Breakfast & lunch	.42
	Bananas	.10
	Donuts	.05
	Soup	.05
	Room	.25
20	Sweat socks	.70
	Breakfast	.30
	Donuts	.10
	Lunch	.20
	Room	.25
	Car fare	.21
21	Meals & room	.55
	Meals	.50
22	Sweater	.50
	Room	2.67
	Meals	.70
23	Meals	.25
24	Pants	2.25
	Haircut	.15
	Suit cleaned	.65
	Meals	.40
	Meals	.42
25	Car fare	.07

10 days in Chicago **21.67**

Nuts! It's too much work to continue keeping accounts!

— For Kodak only —

2 rolls	.34
Postage	.06
1 roll	.25
Postage	.02
1 roll	.30
Pictures	1.44

Development	.40
Total for pictures	2.81

— *Totals* —

July 30		
	Food	2.28
	Other	2.78
	Total	*5.06*
August 27		
	Food	6.90
	Other	8.68
	Total	*15.58*
September 14		
	Food	12.14
	Other	13.88
	Total	*26.02*

— *Money In* —

Sold pants clip	.05
July 16 found	.01
Rode for Jack	.50
Given	.10
Rode for cigarettes	.05
Hart by mail	1.00
Sold tool kit	.35
Sold beer bottles	.60
Sold two books	1.00
Hart by mail	5.00
Wise – work	.35
Total	*9.01*

— *Rickshaw Business* —

Sept.	19	5.95
	20	2.40
	21	5.75

Hart's on his second
million.

The end.

(Erce continued to earn $2 to $3
a day above our expenses to the
end of the Fair.)

Part Two

Chicago to New Orleans
1,500 miles by canoe

HART—WISE ODYSSEY

We started on windy Lake Michigan, our canoe a bit tippy,
And ended at New Orleans, on the mighty Mississippi.
Down the Illinois River, we paddled our way,
Past towns of Florence, Montezuma, and Moscow Bay.

Struck Ol' Miss' at Grafton, where no one knew us,
The current was stronger, all the way to St. Louis.
Two cops there, gave us the eye,
But after some questions, let us go by.

On the *City of Helena*[1], we hitch a ride,
Arrived at Cairo, on the Illinois side.
Rode our thumbs into Missouri, to visit Hart's kin,
Through the Ozark hills, where I'd never been.

Biscuits and gravy, with chicken dinner,
Good friends - good food, no desire to get thinner.
Back to Old Muddy, we had to get along,
In Arkansas, we heard a darky's song.

Rainy and cold, making thirty miles a day,
Once we were lucky, found a barn with some hay.
Ducks and geese, all over the sky,
We found a wounded duck, whose time came to die.

---

[1]*City of Helena*—a paddle-wheel river steamer.

Against wind and rain, and even snow,
On to Memphis, we kept on the go.
Made fifty-nine miles, a good day's run,
Cold as ice, we never saw the sun.

Stopped at Helena (Arkansas), to pick up our mail,
Had dinner with the Johnsons[2], and shared our tale.
Natchez, the next town along our way,
Slept aboard a ferryboat, a good place to stay.   (Out of the
    rain.)

On to Baton Rouge, home of the Kingfish,[3]
To paddle in the moonlight, became our wish.
Finally reached New Orleans, in the sunny south land,
After fifteen hundred miles, we "expected" a band.

It was Christmas Eve, and her name was Jean,[4]
Aboard the *Zarark*[5] of Chicago, she was just sixteen.
On the ship *Oritani*[6], we soon got a berth,
Thus ends my story, for whatever it's worth.

---

[2]Johnsons—owners of the *City of Helena*.

[3]Kingfish—nickname of Huey Long, Governor of Louisiana, 1934.

[4]Jean—daughter of the owners of the *Zarark*.

[5]*Zarark*—a small sailboat we met on the river.

[6]*Oritani*—a small ocean-going freighter.

5

Chicago and the Fair (1934)

The cold rain spattered against the coach's windows as we rode along all night. In the morning the train slowly poked along between many corn fields on low, flat land. We were in Illinois, the Prairie State, but had little idea of where. The poker game continued as usual and maybe had lasted all night for all we knew.

About five that afternoon we arrived on the outskirts of Chicago and could smell a stench miles before we got to the stockyards. What an offensive odor they gave off. We had eaten only bread for breakfast, lunch, and supper, and were anxious to get off the train. As soon as it stopped we grabbed our things, said "goodbye" to the cowboys and walked along beside the tracks until we found the shipping office. There we turned in our passes and asked directions to the nearest YMCA, where we planned to spend the night. Roselawn and

Brooklyn were forgotten about. We were in Chicago and as far as we were going for awhile.

Carrying our bags of clothes, we walked nearly fifty city blocks—mostly through a pretty poor-looking neighborhood —before we found the "Y." A shower was top priority. Afterwards in our room we took stock of our finances and tried to figure out what to do next. We had spent $26.02 on the trip so far (74 days at the rate of 35 cents per day) and had $10.80 left. We would have to conserve, we knew. The YMCA's were our first choice as a place to stay throughout the trip. There we could have a hot shower, usually a swim, and a room with a good bed. Some "Y's" had places to eat also. They were clean and the personnel always helpful to us. The price for a room, although reasonable, was too much for us to stay there continuously, so we asked a clerk if he knew of a cheaper place where we could stay.

"The transient building in the Loop," he replied.

"What's the Loop?" I asked.

"That's the area inside the El," he responded.

"What's the El?" I wanted to know. He knew that we were "hicks from the sticks" but patiently explained that the "El" was an elevated rail transportation system that circled the inner city.

In the morning, after bread and milk for breakfast, we checked our bedrolls at the "Y" and started walking toward the city center—the Loop. It was Sunday, September 16th. We passed several churches where nicely dressed people were entering. If we hadn't had such shabby clothes we might have attended like we would have, had we been home.

On we walked for seventy blocks (about five miles) to the transient building. It at one time had been a store but had been taken over by the city to house the needy. The first floor had an office, kitchen and tables with benches where people could sit to eat. The upper floors were used for sleeping. We stood in line, with other people in the same fix we were, waiting to sign up for a place to stay and free meals. It just happened that we were split up. Erce got a ticket for a room at a nearby cheap hotel and my ticket assigned me to the transient building. That taken care of, we walked about three more miles to the World's Fair. The official title, "Century of Progress International Exposition," we just shortened to "the Fair."

I have seen several World's Fairs since that time, but nothing as extensive as the Chicago one in 1933–34. It extended for miles along the shore of Lake Michigan and included 127 buildings and concessions. A large lagoon, about one mile long, had excursion boats that circled around inside. One of Admiral Richard Byrd's polar sailing ships, tied along the side of a wharf, was there for people to explore. Byrd at the time was on another ship, the *Bear*, in the Antarctic, and his discoveries there were very much in the news.

Beyond the lagoon, land had been leveled to make what was called the Enchanted Island. Many more exhibits, gardens, villages, and clubs, plus the famous Adler Planetarium, were located there. Just outside the fairgrounds one could visit the Shedd Aquarium and the huge Field Museum. Soldier's Field Stadium across from the museum had many events, some of which were free. There was a sky-ride to the Enchanted Island, an illuminated fountain in the lagoon, and several bandstands and stages for outdoor shows. I attended the Fair many times during the six weeks Erce and I were in Chicago, but still couldn't see everything there was to see.

Approaching Soldier's Field that first day we saw some fireworks—as the gate was open, we went inside to see what was taking place. We needed a rest anyway. The "Pageant of Chicago" was being played out on the field with machine-gun fights and lots of fireworks. I didn't understand what was being enacted at first, having missed the start of it, but it did look like a battlefield with a war going on. When the show ended we bought a supper for twenty cents each, then walked to the Fair gate. A man coming out gave Erce a re-enter pass, so he went in.

I waited around awhile, then walked back to the transient building, arriving just two minutes before they locked the doors at midnight. I went upstairs to a floor where perhaps a hundred or more canvas cots were set up. Many were taken, but I found an empty one with a couple of Army blankets folded on it. I spread them out. Taking my pants off, I carefully folded them for a pillow—making sure my wallet was placed directly under my head. It took me awhile to get to sleep under those unfamiliar conditions, but I finally did in spite of the "music" from several snoring men.

In the morning I washed in the community washroom, then went downstairs to stand in line for breakfast. I was handed a bowl of oatmeal with some milk and a cup of coffee. Finding a table with an empty space, I sat down with some older men. They ate without any conversation, and they all looked sad and discouraged. Feeling uncomfortable, I got out of there as soon as I could to look up Erce at his hotel.

He was still asleep, having not gotten in until two. His room—more a stall than a room—had an open top above six feet, and the walls didn't go all the way to the floor. Still he had more privacy than I had had, so for twenty-five cents I rented another stall for the night.

We decided that I should go back to the "Y" to get our toilet articles, then meet at the Fair gate. We would attend the Fair's Constitution Day Celebrations (September 17th) on our second full day in Chicago. For fourteen cents I rode streetcars to the "Y" and to the Fair. I wasn't going to walk the seventy blocks again.

Erce and I paid one dollar each to enter and receive our Constitution Day books, which we later sold for fifty cents

Sept. 7

VENING OUTLOOK, SANTA MONICA, CALIFO[

Santa Monica Boys in Montana
On Bicycle Sight-Seeing Trip

With their cyclometers past the 2,000 mile mark since they left Santa Monica, July 4, Ercell Hart and Kenneth Wise, Santa Monica Sea Scouts who are seeing the world from over the handlebars of their racing bicycles, had reached Great Falls, Mont., last Monday, according to a letter received from the travelers by the Santa Monica Evening Outlook's circulation department in which the Scouts were formerly carriers.

Since leaving Santa Monica the boys have panned for gold and fished for salmon in northern California, worked with timber cutters in Oregon and picked berries on a farm in Washington.

Plan River Canoe Trip

Following the Coast route from Santa Monica, the bikers pedaled their way to Portland, then east on the Columbia river highway, crossed the Rockies and reached Great Falls.

From Great Falls, the boys planned to go to Ft. Benton, where they hoped to exchange their bikes for a canoe which they would launch for a trip down the Mississippi to St. Louis, and from there to Chicago for the Century of Progress. From Chicago, they may turn back to the Mississippi and complete their river trip to New Orleans.

Traveling with only about 2[pounds of luggage each, the Scout[report they frequently are "kidded" about their knee length shorts, bu[find that the shorts are the bes[clothing for riding.

Health Excellent

Most of the time, their limited supply of blankets have been enough. On cold nights, they sometimes have found comfortable ha[stacks owned by a friendly farmer[In a number of towns, they hav[been entertained by the Sea Scout[who have invited the travelers t[spend a day or nigh[in their homes

"Our bikes held up o. k.," th[boys wrote. "The kids up here don'[know what a racing bike is. The[think ours are some old fashione[kind."

Wise is the son of Mr. and Mrs[J. W. Wise, 1912 Euclid street; Har[is the son of Mrs. Mae Hart, 132[Ninth street. Both boys have en[joyed excellent health throughou[the trip.

2 Sea Scouts Tire of Land, Long for Boat

After 2,000-Mile Bicycle Trip Will Trade Wheels for Canoe.

Two sea Scouts, after nearly 2,000 miles of travel on dry land, are anxious to get back on the water again.

Ercell Hart and Kenneth Wise of Santa Monica, Calif., arrived in Great Falls Thursday on two rebuilt racing bicycles. Their cyclometers showed they had traveled 1,968 miles since July 4. In that time they have panned gold in northern California, felled trees in Oregon and worked on a farm in Washington.

Traveling by bicycle, they carry only about 25 pounds of luggage, including sufficient bedding to care for them on all except the coolest nights. When the temperature drops they head for haystacks.

Welcomed by Boy Scouts

Through their connection with the sea Scouts of California, the two youths find welcome at Boy Scout headquarters when on this trip and are staying here at the home of Ralph D. Cook, scout executive.

The next objective of the youthful travelers is to obtain a canoe in exchange for their bicycles, for they intend to proceed as quickly as possible to Fort Benton, where they want to launch their canoe for a trip down the river to St. Louis.

From St. Louis they plan to go to Chicago for the world's fair, then head down the Mississippi by canoe to New Orleans. When they reach the Louisiana metropolis they figure they will have had enough travel by water. They hope to proceed overland back to Santa Monica to resume their college studies.

Make 70 Miles Daily

The youths are well tanned as a result of their long journey. In order to provide freedom of movement in pedaling their bikes, they wear knee-length shorts. When the weather is warm they remove their shirts and have plenty of opportunity to absorb sunshine. They reported they have averaged nearly 70 miles a day since they left Portland and headed inland.

RIVER CANOEISTS WOULD GO ABROAD

After Six Weeks' Paddling to City, Boys Seek Job on Ship

Their spirit of adventure unsatisfied after a canoe trip down the Mississippi river from Chicago to New Orleans, Ercell Hart and Kenneth Wise, 21-year-old California youths, were planning Wednesday to seek a job on a ship which would take them to some foreign country.

The two young men, who arrived here December 24 after a six weeks' trip in a 17-foot open canoe, don't care much where they go, but they are certain that they are not yet ready to go home. At present, they are quartered on the boat of a friend at the Southern Yacht Club.

"We want to sell our canoe," the two said, "and we are going to stay at the yacht club until we do. Then we are going somewhere on some boat as sailors or as deckhands or anything. We hope we get on a ship that will take us to some foreign country. We don't care what country it is."

The friends left Chicago, where Hart had been working at the World's Fair pulling a ricksha, on November 2 and visited relatives in Cairo, Ill., for about two weeks. It cost them $30 to make the trip, they said, and they traveled during the day and camped on the riverbank at night.

"We paddled eight hours a day," they related. "It was pretty cold until we got to Lake Providence, and then it got fairly warm."

The youths live in Santa Monica, Cal., and have been planning their trip for almost two years. They left their homes on July 4 on bicycles and finally got to Chicago. Both are Sea Scouts, and it was their work in the organization that first interested them in a river trip, they said.

each. The attendance that day was the biggest yet. We waddled around in the crowd all day and half the night like 400,000 other fools, but still had a wonderful time trying to see everything in one day. At the lagoon open-air theater we saw a great show of divers, clowns, trained horses, flying-trapeze artists, and beautiful fireworks over the water. For lunch we bought a dozen doughnuts for ten cents and ate them all. At supper time we had chili and beans for twenty cents. We were "living it up."

In the afternoon I saw a friend from Santa Monica in the crowd. "Erce, I just saw Ed Butterworth going the other way."

"Let's slip up behind and give him a surprise." We followed him until the crowd thinned a little, then grabbed him —one on each side.

"Pee Wee! Erce! I never expected to see anyone I knew in this crowd."

"Good to see you, Butter," I said. He was one of our Sea Scout group and a friend for many years. The three of us went around together for the rest of the day and night, exchanging personal news along the way. After getting tired of viewing exhibits, we decided to take in "more sophisticated" entertainment by watching the Sally Rand stage show. Sally's "nude" fan-dance was one of the great attractions of the Fair —especially with the male sector. Ed and Erce paid their fares and walked in. I put my money in front of the man giving out tickets.

He pushed it back to me, saying "Sorry, Sonny, this is an adult show. You'll have to be with your parents to get in."

"Parents? I am nearly twenty-one, I don't need a chaperone," I stated loud enough for people nearby to hear.

"Sorry, you don't look over twelve to me," he persisted.

"Look at my driver's license," I said, poking it at him.

People behind me were getting impatient and were yelling, "Let him in. Let him in."

Finally he gave me a ticket, probably because I was holding up the line and not because he believed me. Erce, with a big grin, asked when I caught up, "What's the trouble, Pee Wee?"

"Do you want to miss the show?" Ed laughingly added. They no doubt knew what had happened.

I was embarrassed, so I just grumbled, "Come on. Let's grab a seat."

Sally did very artistic dances and always had her fans in the right places at the right times. She pleased the crowds and got loud shouts from the men in the audience. Her fame as a fan dancer was made at the World's Fair, and it lasted many years. Later on we learned that she was also a very popular customer of the ricksha boys. After the last show each night one of them would give her a ride to the Fair gate where she, or her escort, would hand a generous tip to the lucky "rikie."

We did many miles on foot seeing the fair that day, had a good time with our friend, and arrived at our hotel about 1:00 AM tired and happy. I never went back to the transient building to sleep or eat. After all, we could get good meals at restaurants for only fifteen cents, and we didn't stay at the cheap hotel any longer than we had to.

The next day we walked to the Chicago Yacht Club near Lake Michigan where we saw a canoe that a couple of young men had just paddled up the Illinois River. From them we learned that one could travel by water all the way from Lake Michigan to the Gulf of Mexico. Suddenly, that became our desire—a good substitute for the Missouri River trip. With that dream in mind we would first have to find jobs to earn some money to buy a canoe. Their canoe was not for sale even if we could have bought it. We would have to find a job soon anyway just to eat.

Erce went to the Fair. He found a place to climb over the fence to avoid paying another dollar to get in. I went to the main post office to see if we had any mail. We didn't. I shopped for pants, but didn't buy any. Instead, I once again traveled to the "Y" where I sewed the rip in my pants. On the way back a delivery man in a truck gave me a ride. We went through a section of the city where only black people lived. It surprised me that it covered such an extensive area. I hadn't realized that Chicago had such a large black population. Back in Santa Monica there were only two black boys in my high school class, so I wasn't used to seeing many people of that race.

That night Erce surprised me by saying, "I got a job, starting tomorrow."

"Great! Doing what?"

"Pulling people around the Fair in a ricksha."

"Think I can get one, too?" I asked.

"Not now, because I had to dish out our last five dollars for a uniform." It was good news and heightened our hopes for later getting a canoe to travel down the rivers, possibly all the way to New Orleans. The bad news was that we had only a buck left. We wouldn't have had the money for the uniform except that Erce had received just that amount of cash, the day before in the mail, from his mother.

In the morning we headed for the Fair again. Erce had been given a pass to get in. I didn't have enough money to pay for a ticket, so I scouted the fence for a likely place to go over it. The six foot, net wire fence was easy to climb and get over, but there were guards to watch out for. Near the south end of the grounds I found an isolated place that looked like a safe place to enter. I went over the fence in a hurry and quickly mingled with the crowd. Then I went into the railroad car exhibit, hoping that no guard had seen me, or I could elude any that had.

After looking around for about twenty minutes, I figured it was safe to leave. I was wrong. On the way out a big fellow grabbed me by the arm and said, "My boss would like to talk to you, young fellow." I knew that I had been caught, so I went along peacefully. In a situation like this I tried to act the age that I looked, which really was about fourteen to sixteen, rather than my true age. The guard didn't loosen his grip on my arm all the way to his lookout building, where I saw that he had a splendid view of the place I had gone over the fence.

In the guard's office a fat man behind a desk had me sit down in a wooden chair in front of him and started to question me. "What's your name?" I gave my right name—because I thought they might ask to look at my I.D. "You ever done this before?"

"No, sir," I answered truthfully.

"You ever going to do it again?"

"No, sir," I said, perhaps not so honestly. Suddenly I felt like I was being electrocuted. Pain went all through my body and I jumped up from my seat about a foot high and yelled, *"Ouch!"* The chair had been wired and someone had shot the juice to me. Wow! What a jolt. Everyone in the room was laughing—except me.

"I guess you're telling the truth or else you never would have sat in that chair." He was right. No one caught a second time would voluntarily go through that experience again. They had their fun, so they let me stay in the Fair with the warning that if they caught me again the punishment would be more severe. Talk about "child abuse"—believe me, I had had it. Today they would be sued for a billion dollars—but I survived and went on to more pleasant things, seeing more of the Fair. I had some free tickets to various shows—given to us on Constitution Day—which I used up. It wasn't as much fun doing things alone. Erce and I had done almost everything together for two months and had gotten accustomed to each other, but I couldn't waste the tickets.

I got back to my stall late that night and Erce still later. He had done real well working on that first day, earning the

$5.00 cost of his uniform with 95¢ left over. We were happy about that. I related my experiences. "Got to be more careful, Pee Wee," he said.

"Yeah, I know." I thought I could still feel the electricity surging through me.

The next day we were off to the Fair again. We went to the north gate which was the closest point of entry from our hotel. Erce yelled, "Good luck" to me as he used his pass to get in.

"I'll see ya," I said as I pondered what to do. There was a newspaper stand near the entrance and I started talking to one of the two boys there. We didn't look too much different in age, I guess.

After awhile he said, "You looking for a way into the Fair?"

"Yeah. I got caught yesterday," and I related my experience.

"Buy one of my special issues and I'll tell you where to get in."

"Is it safe?" I asked.

"No one's been caught there yet."

I paid the twenty-five cents, but told him to keep the paper. I still had enough money left in my pocket to buy some doughnuts for lunch. He told me to go along Soldier's Field to tunnel number seventeen, then go straight over to the fence. I sauntered down the walk and found the place all right. There was a big hole under the fence that I had no trouble getting through. It looked like many other lads had used that place to get in also. I entered between the Swedish and Czechoslovakian exhibits, not really popular attractions, where there weren't many people or guards to see me. I used that same entrance several more times and never did get caught. I had a "season's pass," and for only the price of a newspaper. I high-tailed it over to the ricksha office, arriving just in time to see Erce going out with a customer. He gave me a surprised look and then a smile. I asked the boss for a job, giving Hart's name for a reference.

"Boy, you're just too small."

"I can pull a ricksha. The Japanese and Chinese aren't very big either and they do it," I insisted.

"I know. I'd like to help you out," he politely said, "but we're supposed to hire college track men—so I just can't take you on."

I asked if he knew of any other jobs that I might get, but he didn't, so I went on to see more of the Fair and inquire about work at nearly every place. At noon I went out on the rock breakwater at the north end of the lagoon to look at Lake Michigan while eating some doughnuts. Before long I was kicked off of there. My job hunting had been unsuccessful, so I was pretty disgusted. Erce didn't make as much that day—only $2.40, but he made more than I, which, although he never complained, made me feel like I wasn't doing my share.

The following morning I got up late. Erce had gone to work. I went to the post office and found we each had a fat letter from home. Mine made me feel a bit homesick because I was so far away from my family. Winter was coming on and I was 2,000 miles from home. The other one, from Erce's grandmother who lived in Missouri, he was happy to receive. He had written to her that we might come to visit after the Fair. I guess "Missouri" reminded me of the river again, because that afternoon I made a visit to the Yacht Club again, hoping that I might either get a lead on a boat ride down the river or find a canoe for sale. I did find the latter, but I thought the $35.00 price was too high. I talked to some Sea Scouts I met there about their activities, boats, and organization for a time before returning to the flophouse where we still resided. It rained hard during the night, but Erce worked through it until 4:00 AM. He made $5.75 and felt that he had earned it. He had tired legs and feet.

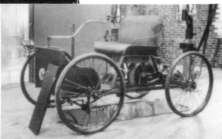

Snapshots from the 1934 World's Fair—
pavilions and the first Ford car.

Newt Young in Erce's "rik" and Ercell
in front of the "Streets of Shanghai."
World's Fair, Chicago—1934.

About a week after Erce got his job, we had saved enough money to afford to move to a rooming-house nearer the Fair. We went in with another "Rik-fellow," Newton Young, a tall track-man from the University of Missouri, to share expenses. Our room had three beds, but no hot water or keys for the door. At $4.00 a week we felt that it was a gyp. A week later we moved to a nicer place. For only a dollar more a week, we had many more conveniences, keys, hot water, plus very friendly landlords.

One day I took a long walk north to Lincoln Park where I found a canoe for sale, also for thirty-five dollars. Out on the lake many boats were sailing to good advantage under a brisk breeze. I would have liked to have been on one of them. Back in southern California I had done considerable sailing, even worked on a yacht for awhile, and I missed the thrill and freedom felt while letting the wind power one's boat along.

In the afternoon I returned by way of the Fair and went in under the fence again. Once more I tried to get a ricksha-pulling job. "Pee Wee," the boss said, "You haven't grown a bit taller since the last time you were here." He knew me and had learned my nickname from Erce. There just weren't any jobs available because the Fair was sort of winding down as the season progressed toward the closing day.

By chance I did work for one afternoon, but quit because thirty-five cents was all I received for pay—besides it was a horrible job. I think you will agree. I was about to go into a place called the "Chamber of Tortures" to see what it was like when the guy who was "barking in the people" surprisingly asked me if I wanted a job.

"What doing?" I inquired.

"Can you give a talk?"

"I suppose so."

"Follow me, then," he said as he put on a black cloak and went inside where people were milling around looking at various ancient torture devices. On display were the rack, guillotine, water torture where water slowly dripped on a prisoner's firmly held forehead, stocks, a platform with sharp nails on which a person was forced to lie, and other things I can't remember. The man gave a short speech telling the names and how the devices were used, plus a little history about them. "This is the rack, a medieval instrument of torture. The prisoner was placed on this wooden frame, his arms and legs tied down, which were then stretched. It was generally used to extort confessions from a victim. When the pain became unbearable he usually confessed or fainted and. . . ."

About this time someone in the audience gasped, "Oh! How horrible." His talk went on like that about the other devices and then he asked for donations of money for the support of the exhibit. It was supposed to be a free show. At least that is what he said when calling people in.

To me he said, "Got the idea?" and without further ado or an answer from me, he flipped the black robe over my shoulders, saying "I'll get you an audience." He did just that and I had to give the speech without any more training. I stumbled through it somehow, but I forgot about the donation part—at least the first time—and just said, "Put your money in the cup as you go out." The boss got complaints about that.

At the end of the day I received a percentage of the donations, which was small indeed. I believe people didn't want to support horror. I think his previous helper quit for the same reason that I did—being underpaid.

In the evening, for the second time since being at the Fair, I went to the show at the lagoon theater. The lighting effects over the water and in the fountain were beautiful— but the big, full moon rising over the lake made the little show rather insignificant in comparison. The flying-trapeze men and women did their usual thing, but I saw something unusual, too—ponies trained to dive. From a platform twenty-five feet above the lagoon, they jumped to splash into the water and swim out. I hadn't seen anything like that before.

The last days of September and the first in October were truly an "Indian summer" with sunny, warm days which we enjoyed. One day I walked many miles along the lake front through pretty parks lined by nice homes of brick or stone. Also I stopped at the University of Chicago to visit a friend, "Beefer," the name we called him, who was our camp doctor at Catalina. He was in his last year of study before getting a degree.

"What a surprise," he said. "Pee Wee, what are you doing in Chicago?"

"Came to see you and the Fair," I responded, giving equal importance to both. We had a good visit before I went to the "Y" to pick up Erce and my bedrolls that we had left there weeks before.

Sunday, the last day of September, Erce stayed home for a day of rest, the first he had had since starting work, and we had a good dinner together for a change. I had bought some red apples for a dollar fifty per bushel and we had a couple for dessert. He had been working so hard that we hadn't seen very much of each other. I told him that I had located a canoe that could probably be purchased for twenty-five dollars. I asked him if he thought we should get it and if we could afford it. He handed me ten dollars and said, "Sure, make a down payment with this, and when the Fair is over we'll paddle down the rivers."

"Sounds good to me. I just wanted to be sure that we had the same idea." After three months together we were still buddies.

Four days later I did offer twenty-five dollars for the canoe that had a thirty-five dollar price tag on it. The owner, a pleasant fellow, hesitated only slightly before saying "It's a deal." We shook hands on it and I made a down payment.

The canoe appeared to be sound but needed a coat of paint —which I planned to give it. It had sponsons (air chambers along the rails of the canoe for stability) which made it a bit heavier than I liked, but they did add a margin of safety that we otherwise wouldn't have had because we couldn't afford any life jackets. Its length of seventeen feet was about right for two men with the small amount of luggage that we had left from our bike trip and the additional supplies we would need to purchase for a fall and winter trip down the rivers. At point it looked like our planned canoe voyage was "for real."

On the two following days I visited the famous Chicago Field Museum. It had in it everything that ever existed, I thought, from mammoth skeletons to birch bark canoes. Like the Fair, I couldn't see it all. The next day I spent trying to get a job of any kind, but had no luck at all.

On October 8th I went with some more money to see Al Markham, the canoe owner. He was a trusting fellow, offering to let me take the canoe even though I was five dollars short of full payment.

"When are you leaving on your trip?" he asked.

"About the 1st of November—when the Fair is over."

"I would like to go along with you fellows," he said, "even though it will be a little late in the year, and you may run into some really cold, bad weather."

"I hadn't thought about that—except for rain," I told him. Indeed, being from California, I didn't realize that November in the Chicago area could have some severe weather with freezing temperatures and even heavy snow fall.

Al helped me launch the canoe into Lake Michigan and I paddled out through some small waves to fairly calm water. I had about ten miles to travel to the Fair lagoon boat shed where Erce had arranged with the manager to store our canoe. On the way I discovered that the canoe handled very well and that its canvas cover kept it from leaking. She was dry and tidy, so to speak. It had been a long time since I had paddled and it felt good to be riding in a canoe again. On the lake I was away from the crowd and felt free. That made me think of Catalina and the good trips I had made there with Al Snyder.

In a little over two hours I came to the lagoon entrance where a big chain stretched across from side to side, but the sag in the chain left a few inches of water over it in the middle. I skimmed over the chain with ease. I had just about reached the location of Byrd's ship when a lagoon cruise boat cut me off.

"Hey, you can't come in here," the boatman shouted. When I explained that I had permission, he let me pass. After one more such encounter, I made it to the boat shed where I pulled the canoe up onto the landing and turned it over to dry. The boat concession manager helped me carry it to the back, out of the way, saying, "It looks like a fine canoe." I agreed.

A little later, on the fairgrounds, I met Erce looking for a customer, with an empty ricksha rolling along behind him. "I just put *Miss Gullabalonia* in the boat shed," I said.

"You what?"

"I brought the canoe back," I laughed. We both agreed that odd name would have to go. *Islander*, after our Sea Scout ship, would be more appropriate we thought.

October 14 was noteworthy for the fact that I put on a clean shirt. The next day the weather turned colder. The attendance at the Fair had dropped, but Erce still made some money. He even got a big tip from Sally Rand one night after taking her to the gate. He told me that she was wearing an expensive looking fur coat—without her fans.

I paid the last five dollars for the canoe, then busied myself painting her a bright emerald green, covering *Miss Gullabalonia* in the process. On her bow I lettered *ISLANDER S.S.S.—16*, and on the stern painted *Chicago to New Orleans*. After that we were committed—we had to make it to that fair city in the sunny southland. The manager of the lagoon boats had secured a pass for me so that I didn't have to go in under the fence any more. Maybe they wanted to save wear and tear on the fence, but anyway I was relieved because I didn't want to get caught again.

One day I made a grub-box for the canoe out of an apple-box I found. It cost only ten cents for some nails and a pair of hinges. In it we would have a place for all our food, cooking gear, log book, and other things. The top folded back to make a table in camp. With a canoe we could carry a much heavier load than we could on bikes. After I bought us some slickers and waterproofed our sleeping bags, we were nearly ready to travel.

October 31st, the last day of the Fair and Hallowe'en, Erce described it in our log book thus:

> Space and time are too short to write a daily account of my six weeks working at the Century of Progress pulling a ricksha. I enjoyed every day, had lots of experiences I hope to remember. I met many people among whom I found several good friends. The last night was a Hallowe'en celebration supreme. A record crowd thronged the grounds, all in search of souvenirs, and many bent on destruction. The resultant damage amounted to several thousand dollars. We quit work at 8:00 PM, received our checks and bade farewell. I hope we may have a reunion sometime. Many good fellows.

It is strange how things like that actually work out sometimes. Erce told me that he did meet with a couple of the ricksha "boys" many years after the Fair—Newton Young and Al Lindsey.

6

Lake Michigan to Cairo

The Fair was over. We had a canoe and a little money extra. All we needed was to stock up on supplies, so we went to a grocery to fill our grub-box with a good supply of food for our start down the rivers. I remember the first time we looked for a grocery store in Chicago, we couldn't find one, and had to ask somebody where to go. Given directions, we finally found the store and the grocery department "hidden away" on the eleventh floor. That seemed strange to us, being used to ground level stores. Big cities do things differently we decided.

We had an enjoyable farewell dinner with our rooming-house managers, Mr. and Mrs. Ken Smith, the evening of November 1st—our plan was to leave the next morning. I showed them a map of the Illinois Waterway System that I had picked up at the U.S. Engineer's office a few days before.

Mr. Smith, after looking over our proposed route, said, "That's a long way to paddle a canoe. How long will it take?"

"If we can manage thirty-five miles per day, we should make the 1,525 miles to New Orleans by the middle of December," Erce replied, "barring we have no trouble."

"You forgot our planned side trip in Missouri to see your Grandfather," I reminded him.

"Okay, then we should get there by Christmas."

Our way from Lake Michigan began in the Chicago River, continuing through the dredged channel of the Sanitary and Ship Canal to the Des Plaines River, which becomes the Illinois River on down where the Kankakee comes in. From there it holds that name all the rest of the way to the Mississippi River at the town of Grafton. The entire length of 327 miles was open to barge and boat traffic, and had been formally opened, June of 1933, only a little over a year before our trip. During one sixty mile stretch the river drops 139 feet, and before the five dams and locks were built in that section, there were many shallow rapids and navigation was not practicable. The river current ranged from one to three miles per hour. On the Mississippi River the current was slightly faster, but it didn't seem to increase our daily average very much.

In the morning with the weather a bit blustery, Newton Young and Al Lindsey, "Rik" buddies of Erce's, helped us carry our gear to our canoe at the Fair lagoon. The food box was heavy, but the rest of our stuff was light because we didn't have very much in the way of camping gear—really just some extra clothes, our bed rolls, and a piece of canvas to cover them in the canoe. There were two paddles that came with the canoe, and that's all. We could have used a tent, shovel, axe, ground cloth, pads, an extra paddle, and more canvas. It would have been nice to have had more blankets in our sleeping bags—as they just consisted of the single blankets we had used during the summer on our bike trip. We found out as the days got colder that some long-johns would have been nice too.

The fairgrounds looked deserted as we passed through to the boat shed. About the only people around were some men who had bought lagoon boats and were getting them ready to travel. We stowed our gear in the canoe and with a last look around and handshakes with Al and Newt, we "cleared" for New Orleans.

"Send me a post card," Newt yelled as we started off.

"Don't tip over," Al added. "Good luck, voyageurs."

With Erce in the stern and me in the bow we paddled out of the lagoon into a stiff breeze blowing across the lake. The temperature stood at 34° and the water was rough. Before we covered the four miles to the start of the Chicago River we took a few waves over the rail, but all was calm once we got past the entrance. There wasn't much current with us, still we could paddle along pretty fast on the smooth water. We could hear the cars and trucks on the bridges crossing the river at almost every city street, as we continually went under them. We counted more than fifty before the canal ended. The river lasted for six miles, then we were in the straight channel of the Sanitary Canal.

It wasn't any fun until we got past the city with its noise and smells. Sewage from the slaughter houses dumped in the canal made it especially stinky. I longed for the clean air and water we hoped to find farther on—like I had known at Catalina. We paddled until dark and still hadn't found a suitable spot to camp. The only place we could find was near a town called Romeo where we pulled out under a highway bridge, and after a struggle getting the canoe up the steep bank to a halfway level spot, we spent the night. There would be better days, we hoped, but at least we had made about thirty-five miles and were glad to be out of Chicago.

The wind whipped the rain on us during that miserable night. In the morning we built a fire and partially dried out while cooking and eating breakfast. We started paddling against the wind and rain, but didn't make much headway. The two locks we encountered also slowed us down.

The first one came into view at Lockport just a few miles below where we spent the night. There we paddled into the open lock and waited until another boat came along before the operators would seal us in to lower the water about forty feet to the lower level of the canal. When they opened the lower gates we floated out with the current caused by the water level in the lock still being higher than the water outside. We had to paddle hard to keep the canoe from swirling around in the current. The operators were not used to such a small craft as our canoe going through the lock. A few miles farther we came to the end of the uninteresting canal and started down the Des Plaines River which was much wider and had pleasant shore lines, with trees and grass coming down to the water's edge.

Even though we didn't enjoy traveling in a canal it truly was, from a historical standpoint, quite famous. In early years of the country (1600) French fur traders envisioned such a waterway so as to be able to travel all the way from Quebec to New Orleans. Long afterwards (1848) the Illinois and Michigan Canal was completed, opening up Chicago and the rest of the midwest to further settlement. At the time the hand-dug canal with its hand-operated wooden locks was an engineering masterpiece. This is not to be confused with the newer dredged ship canal opened in 1933 as mentioned before. The old canal headquarters building at Lockport houses the country's Historical Society Museum's collections of canal memorabilia. The second lock, Brandon Road, we reached at the little town of Joliet, and paddled right on in. The lock operator looked at us in surprise for a minute then said, "What's the tonnage of the *Islander*?"

"How about eighty-five pounds?" Erce replied.

"Do you expect me to let all this water out just for an eighty-five pound canoe?" he asked.

"We could portage if it's too much trouble," I offered, although a slight smile on his face gave him away.

"Nah! I don't expect any more boats today anyway." With that remark he closed the gates behind us and started letting the water out while we were lowered all by ourselves about thirty-five feet. It was kind of an eerie feeling, like being slowly dropped into a well with the sky getting smaller all the time. Again we were let out with a swish, but we had learned to stay back from the gates a little way, so we didn't have any trouble. There were no fees charged for going through the government owned and operated locks.

A mile below town we came to a yacht club where several boats were moored in the river. It had started raining again and we were looking for a shelter for the night. We both got the idea at the same time of tying the canoe to one of the motor boats. Erce brought the canoe alongside of the biggest one and I grabbed on. The boat's cockpit was dry, being enclosed with canvas all around. I climbed in and Erce handed me the bedrolls, then some food. We bunked on the cushions for the night. It had taken much time going through the locks, so we hadn't made many miles that day, but we had finally gotten out of the long canal. Thinking about the day's events, Erce said, "Well, we have seen Romeo and Joliet, wonder what kind of show tomorrow will bring?"

"Go to sleep, Dreamer," I said. "Let tomorrow take care of itself."

The town of Joliet was named after Shakespeare's heroine, and not as I first thought after Louis Joliet who in 1673 with Father Marquette and five assistants were the first white men to visit the Illinois River area. Then came LaSalle, who did have a town named after him. Later "explorers," like us, didn't have a chance of getting a town named after them.

"**W**hat the hell are you doing here?" the watchman wanted to know as he poked his head into the cockpit as we were getting out of bed. We had heard his skiff bump alongside and thought he had seen our canoe and had come out to investigate. We explained our situation of the night before to him. He looked around to see that we hadn't broken anything and then said, "I'll let you go because I have to get this boat ready for the owner who will be here soon." We hastened to make a departure, not even taking time to mop out a half inch of water that had rained into the canoe during the night. We just put our bedrolls in and shoved off—all the time thanking the man for the night's lodging. On down the river a bit we bailed the water out and later stopped to cook our breakfast.

The river was more interesting than before, with curves and islands to maneuver around. We passed the mouth of the Kankakee River—so we knew we had reached the Illinois River at the confluence. Just before we got to the Dresden lock and dam, a World's Fair lagoon boat caught up to us. The two young fellows aboard brought their craft close by. "Hello canoeists, want a ride?" one shouted.

"Sure thing, and thanks." As the wind was against us, we gladly accepted—besides that was our first chance to ride in one of those boats. We hauled all our stuff, including the canoe, aboard and headed for the lock. They had seen us leave the Fair lagoon and wondered where they might see us again, they told us. They were delivering the boat to a buyer in Davenport, Iowa. We went along about three times as fast as we would have paddling the canoe.

Every five or ten miles we came to little towns along the shore, perhaps like Indian villages had been before the white man came. We passed Morris, Seneca, and Marseilles, where another lock had to be negotiated. Below the lock and with a little more river under our boat, we came to Ottawa. The strange names of the towns, especially the Indian ones, were intriguing and made us wonder about their naming.

Just before we came to Utica another lock appeared, the third drop for the day. Its name, Starved Rock, really made me curious. From a lock employee I learned that many years before a great battle had taken place between the local Illinois tribe and the invading Ottawas. A remnant of the Illinois took refuge on the rocky promontory where the explorer LaSalle had once built a fort. They were besieged there and held by their enemies until they starved to death. The story even has a romantic touch. . . . a beautiful Indian maiden had flung herself from the rock into the river after seeing her lover killed. Nowadays at the Waterway Visitor Center, Starved Rock State Park, one can watch tow boats push barges through the lock and even steer one's own tow of barges through the lock in a computer simulation. The Center is open mid-March to mid-December. (Information: (815) 667−4054)

At Peru we tied up alongside of a government Q-boat for the night. The Q, or Quarter-boat, was a barge with a house on it, used by the men in the U.S. Engineer's Division to eat and live in while they worked on the river. It could be moved to their work place—a dredging site, for example. It carried supplies for their work and living necessities. Erce and I slept aboard the Fair boat, keeping dry under a tarp stretched over the canoe. It rained most of the night.

We traveled more than fifty miles that day—a helpful boost toward getting along and out of the cold country. The date, November 4th, made it another anniversary of our start from California four months before. After the rain we had a clear and windless morning. The two young fellows, having slept in a hotel, came back and suggested that we ride a few more miles with them to where they had to take the Illinois-Mississippi Canal cut-off toward Iowa. Together we motored on for thirteen miles to their junction and then were let off. We waved good-by to them and the *Morton Downey*, the name of the lagoon boat.

That day was bright and beautiful with the sun warming us. The river was glassy smooth, making paddling fun. Birds were singing or calling to each other. It sounded like an aviary. We began to really enjoy the canoeing for the first time. The riverbanks and hills were covered with trees mostly bare of leaves, but some with colorful autumn foliage still hanging on. The ground was blanketed with fallen colors of red, yellow, orange and brown.

We drifted while we made and ate sandwiches for lunch. Then we paddled many miles, passing the little villages of Hennepin, Henry, and Lacon before camping on a wooded bank. We built a campfire to cook a stew and to keep us warm. The night was clear and we slept well with leaves for a mattress and more for a cover. The river ran in a southwesterly direction toward the Mississippi River, and we were thirty-five miles nearer Grafton, the place where we would join it.

The dawn broke clear and cold. We paddled about a mile to Chillicothe where we bought some grub and even took time to write some cards home. By the time we got to Lake Peoria, a wide part of the river, the wind blowing directly upstream stopped our progress. We tied the canoe to a little boat landing and had a walk ashore to wait for the blow to ease. As we wandered among the trees, I tried to visualize how it had been along the river before the white man came to spoil it. In my imagination I could see the buffalo, turkeys and other wildlife that once existed there and Indians in canoes on the river coming to their villages along the shores. It would never be like that again, as "civilization" with more and more people moved there and the towns continued to grow bigger. It was good to have a walk, but we didn't want to leave the canoe alone for very long. By the time Erce and

I returned to the lake the wind had quieted down some, so we paddled across the lake to camp near a place named Spring Bay. We hadn't made ten miles all day.

The next day was better traveling. We made it to the end of the lake and back into the river at Peoria in a couple of hours. The riverbank there was covered with a community of house boats. Some were in the water, and others, no longer fit for service, propped up high on shore with pilings, still served as homes. Things have changed greatly since we were there during the Depression. Now just south of Peoria at Dickson Mounds stands a state museum. It has been built over the burial site of an ancient Indian village. There exhibits tell how the Indians once lived, farmed and hunted in the Illinois River Valley. We passed Pekin and Kingston Mines before camping near Coon Hollow Island. We had made an average day's run of about thirty miles, calculated from our map.

November 8th we passed more towns with interesting names like Liverpool and Havana, but only stopped at any of these places if we needed something. We camped on seven-mile-long Grand Island across from Bath—another odd name for a town I thought. We would have liked a bath, but the river was too cold. Some towns were named after Indian tribes, like Peoria and Ottawa, and the river after the Illinois people. Others were named, by the early settlers, after foreign places they had lived before coming to the wilderness.

We had good paddling the next day in less settled country, passing only one town—Beardstown. Just before getting there we saw a rather large tributary join the Illinois from the east. From our little map we found it was the Sangamon River. Later I learned that Abe Lincoln had built a flat-boat, with the help of two other young men, and launched it on the Sangamon near a place now called Springfield. They then loaded it with barrels of pork, corn, hogs, and other provisions for a journey down that river to the Illinois, and on down it and the Mississippi River to New Orleans. I am sure we made our trip much faster in the *Islander* than Abe did in his flat-boat. It was interesting to learn that we followed the same route that he did many years earlier. Now many years later Springfield, considered to be Abraham Lincoln's home town, has grown and changed. The Old Statehouse, where he taught law, has been restored. The only home he owned has recently undergone renovation. About twenty miles northwest of Springfield is a re-created log town where Lincoln spent many years. New Salem State Park has stores where he worked and a tavern where he ate, along with homes that he visited.

The current helped some, and we paddled hard to keep warm in the frosty morning. The country had rolling hills that we kept watching for deer, but didn't see any. Along the river banks the hardwood trees colorfully displayed their gaudiness by dripping a spectrum of leaves into the dark water below as the frost caused their leaves to drop. We came to LaGrange lock and dam, which was only six feet high. We hadn't seen any upstream markers as warnings about the dam but could plainly see the lock so pulled over. "I wouldn't care to go over that dam in a canoe," I remarked to a young fellow at the lock.

With a southern accent, he slowly responded by saying, "They have did it! But not apurpose."

We went on a few miles and camped at Moore's Towhead Island. Our map showed that we had seventy-six miles more to reach the Mississippi River, which meant we had traveled 271 miles from Chicago. We didn't have any schedule and were just trying to make as many miles a day as we comfortably could.

The next day after passing the towns of Naples, Florence, Montezuma, Bedford and Pearl, our camp was only forty-one miles from the Big River—we had made another thirty-five-mile day's run. Part of the day we had a tail wind and had held up a canvas for a sail. That was fun as long as we stayed upright. We thought of Al Lindsey's warning the day we left—"Don't tip over."

A little ice had formed at the water's edge during the night and it was cold the next morning, November 11th, Armistice Day (Veteran's Day now), as we started out. We were paddling hard to keep warm when we came to the lock and dam below Kempsville. The lock-man hollered at us, "You'd better paddle like hell before it gets cold up here." Evidently he had seen our "Chicago to New Orleans" sign on the *Islander* and was urging us on.

"I think it's cold already," I yelled back.

"Not yet, but it's coming," he responded.

It was only a short drop in the lock and he put us right through. The sun shown brightly, yet we could see our breath in the cold air even at noon. We had the river to ourselves most of the day and sang songs such as "Blow the Man Down" and other sea ditties to the rhythm of our paddles for hours. About 4:00 PM we sighted a Three-C camp with several drab buildings up from the river on a small hill, so we made our camp for the night on the river bank just below theirs. We still had seven miles to go before reaching the Mississippi River and couldn't make it before dark anyway.

We had sharp eyes when it came to finding CCC camps. I don't believe we missed any along our route, but we hadn't seen the welcome sight of one since we had left Oregon. We took soap, razor, and towels from our pack, then walked to the camp. A young "First Looie" who appeared to be in charge let us use the washroom and invited us to dinner. We shaved with hot water for a change—what bliss. We dined scrumptiously, enjoying the holiday dinner very much, then visited with the men in camp. They were all World War I veterans and most were feeling in high spirits because of the sixteenth anniversary of the Armistice. We learned a lot about the first World War before we left for our camp that night. We hadn't expected to run into a Three-C camp in Illinois, but were happy that we had. Meals that we cooked were mainly stews and pretty poor compared to what we were served there.

Frost covered the ground like snow as we made our way to the CCC camp for breakfast. They had invited us back. After eating, some of the men walked with us to the river to see our canoe. We felt good and full of anticipation as we loaded the canoe and started off for our last day on the Illinois River and the first day on "Ol' Miss." After an hour of strong paddling we came to Grafton, the town at the mouth of the Illinois, and then we saw the Mississippi River. My! It looked so big and our canoe seemed so small. What a great day and one that we had dreamed about all the way from Chicago.

We didn't have any charts of the Mississippi but planned to get some at St. Louis, which we had heard was about thirty-eight miles down river and on the other side. We

Ken—where the Illinois River joins the Mississippi.

thought we might make it before the day ended. After a short stretch on land while looking around town, we were back in the canoe and striking out boldly for the middle of the river where the current would be fastest. We were eager to get to St. Louis because we were pretty certain of having some mail there. We ate lunch in the canoe that day to save time, besides it was quite a distance to shore from the center of the river. At one place where the river seemed wider than usual we thought we discerned the mouth of the Missouri River about a half mile away. Also, the current seemed faster and the water was muddy after that. Had we come down the Missouri we might have arrived at this very same place about the same time, and we might have headed on toward St. Louis and New Orleans just like we were doing.

We could see St. Louis in the distance when we came to an island where we thought it prudent to camp for the night, because it would have been dark before we could get there. In getting ashore we were almost swept onto a sandbar just below the surface, which could have been no trouble or could have tipped us over depending on how we hit it—point or broadside. While paddling we both generally kept looking ahead, but as bowman it was my duty to sight and report any possible danger, and Erce's job to steer clear. When I saw the ripple in the water ahead, I yelled, "Bar ahead" and Erce, with my help, swung the canoe around so we were heading upstream.

"Paddle for shore," Erce commanded. The current was pretty strong, maybe three or four miles per hour, at that place and we worked hard to keep off the bar and to get ashore—which we managed to do. We found that the Big River had tricks that we would have to guard against. With a big fire glowing we felt like a couple of Huckleberry Finns on our private island in the middle of the Mississippi River. The lights of St. Louis across the reflecting water indicated to us that it was a big place, and would have a YMCA that we would want to visit and definitely have a post office. We had traveled about forty miles that day, and had safely completed the first leg of our journey—the Illinois River.

The next morning it didn't take us long to get to St. Louis because we were helped by the current and a strong tail wind. We docked at Mound City Boat Works near Ead's Bridge and then struck out for the post office. There we received some letters and a package for my birthday, which was still four days away, and we left a forwarding address of New Orleans. We found the U.S. Division of Engineer's office and got charts of the river as far as Cairo, Illinois. We dropped into a public rest room and were washing up when two plain-clothes officers found us and started asking questions. Maybe we looked plenty tough, anyway suspicious in our outfits of dungarees and no shirts. After all, St. Louis was a big city, and evidently drifters were being watched closely.

"Where you fellows from?" they wanted to know.

"Originally from California and recently from Chicago," Erce replied.

"What you doing in St. Louis?"

"Picking up our mail," I said—showing it to them.

"Where you going?"

"New Orleans." Erce showed them the river charts.

"How you traveling?"

"By canoe," we both answered.

"I guess you're not the guys we're looking for."

Before they left I asked them for directions to the YMCA. I don't know if the cops informed the "Y" that we were coming or not, but when we got there we were received like two long-lost bold adventurers or something like that. The secretary suggested that we give our trip story to the editor of the *St. Louis Globe-Democrat*.

After a swim and shower we did go to the newspaper office. They received our story and took a photograph of us, giving us two extra prints. We looked pretty young in the picture and not very tough, I thought. I didn't read the story they wrote until fifty-four years later after I sent for a copy of the November 14th, 1934 article from the paper. It was there all right, but was really mixed up as far as correct reporting went—which mattered little then and none at all now. By the time we got back to the river it was too late to start out. The boat works boss kindly let us sleep in one of his yachts for the night.

Democrat.

November Globe-Democrate

November 13, 1934   St. Louis, Missouri

BOYS HERE ON LONG JOURNEY IN CANOE

Ercell Hart and Kenneth Wise, both 21, of Santa Monica, Cal., arrived in St. Louis last night to interrupt a canoe trip which started in Chicago November 2. They will leave today for New Orleans.

The boys left home July 4 after completing junior college and rode to Great Falls, Mont., on bicycles. En route they worked on farms in California, felled trees in Oregon and did odd jobs in Washington. From Montana they went to Chicago on a cattle train, having been engaged to tend some stock.

The boys arrived in Chicago in September and Ercell obtained employment pulling rickshaws at the Century of Progress Exposition. They are now en route to New Orleans, which they expect to make by easy stages and then ship for California on a boat. Both are Sea Scouts. They spent last night at the Downtown Y.M.C.A.

In the morning we walked up town to a grocery store and stocked up on food for our trip on down the river to Cairo. We had seen enough of St. Louis to satisfy us so shoved off as soon as we got back. We skimmed along close to the waterfront, where a large colony of riverside shacks were built of all sorts of salvaged materials, from flattened tin cans to old car license plates. On our way from St. Louis we cut in front of a railroad car barge headed towards town. Although we were out of his way in time, the old Mississippi "mud-turtle" skipper didn't like our action at all. From his pilot house window he told us our present characteristics, our pedigree, and chances for Heaven in very definite and unflattering terms. We let his words fly in the breeze and continued to paddle on down the river. We had a stretch of two hundred miles southeast to reach Cairo, where the big Ohio River joins the Mississippi.

Although the weather was cold, we kept warm paddling all day, stopping at noon to stretch and eat our lunch. In the evening we came to a small wing-dam. It extended out in the river a short distance to divert the current and protect the land behind it from washing away. We rounded it a little too close to its end where the current took us for a little dip and circle ride we hadn't expected. In the future we kept farther out from the ends of dams. It made a calm place to camp be-hind the dam, so we pulled ashore. After a supper of chicken and noodle soup, we made beds of reeds and grass. We were expecting another cold night. We were camping in the state of Missouri. I had never been there before, and it had been seventeen years since Erce had left there as a young boy with his folks.

The frost in the morning made it difficult for us to get out of our bags, so we had another late start in the canoe. With Missouri on our right and Illinois on the left we rode the wide river watching the spectacle of water, clouds, birds, river steamers, and shore lines come and go. Near day's end we came to a river-sternwheeler tied to some trees along the bank. Her name, *City of Helena*, showed from a sign on the pilot house. We asked a couple of black fellows standing on the lower deck if we could come aboard. "Shore," they said and they helped us make a landing next to the paddle wheel, where we could get on easily.

We tied the canoe alongside and climbed up. Later, after we met and talked awhile to the captain-owner, Mr. Warren Johnson, he invited us to haul our canoe on board and ride with them to Cairo. We accepted gladly, because we thought it would be a great experience, and it was. They tied up at night to get some sleep because other than the three black deck hands, Warren, his wife, and mother (the pilot) were the only crew.

The *City of Helena* had a decommissioned USDE snagboat, the *J. M. Macomb*, tied on front. They were taking it to Helena (Arkansas), their home port. The old boat had seen many years of service cleaning the river channel of logs and snags, but had been replaced by a newer one. Erce and I had private staterooms with spring beds to sleep on—what class! During the next day we each had a trick at the big wheel in the pilot house steering the river boat as we rode in style down the middle of the great river.

"You ever been on a river boat before?" Warren asked.

"First time, and we surely are enjoying it," I told him.

"Well look her over then," he said.

We did as he suggested by walking both decks from stem to stern, where the big paddle-wheel slapped the water with a regular beat, powered by a big engine. The blacks were engaged in a game of dice on the empty cargo deck. The river was old stuff to them, but Erce and I watched every turn and bend—afraid we might miss something. The lower deck had the steam engine, boiler and cargo area. On the second deck were cabins and a dining room. Above that was the little square pilot house with windows on all four sides, where a clear view of the river, obstructed only by two smoke stacks, could be had. Most everything was painted white including the wooden railing around the cabin deck.

Again that night, under the direction of the captain, the deck hands tied the steamer to trees along the shore. We had supper and a pleasant evening visiting with the Johnsons. The river had been their work place and home most of their lives and they didn't want to trade it for any other. "A good life," they said. At that moment, I thought that I might like to do the same.

Steaming down the river in the morning we anxiously looked ahead for signs of Cairo. Along the river the local people pronounced it "Care-oh." We were passing many small and big islands on one side or the other, depending upon where the main channel had been marked. There were marker signs on shore to help keep us in the center or deepest part of the channel. The river made a big bend to head back north for several miles. When we started south again it wasn't very long before we came in sight of Cairo. The city had been built on a long neck of land between the Mississippi and Ohio Rivers. Wharves lined the shore and Warren steered the steamer toward an unoccupied dock, where she would take on fuel oil.

We had made the trip from St. Louis in much shorter time than we had expected, letting the steamer do the paddling most of the way.

The Author—52 years later

Ozark Frolic

When the ship was tied and a gangplank put down, Erce and I hauled our canoe and gear ashore while the *City of Helena* took on fuel and water. Soon her whistle blew, the lines thrown off, and she started on down the river, but we would see her again. As she pulled out Mr. Johnson extended an invitation to us. "Come see us in Helena."

"We will. We will," I shouted and waved farewell. Had we not planned a trip into the middle of Missouri to visit Hart's relatives, we could have gone on with them. I'll never forget the day I arrived at Cairo, because it was November 17th, my birthday. Erce later wrote in our log book, "Kenny this day came of age—didn't think he'd ever make it."

We stored the *Islander* in a warehouse on the dock where a warehouse man said that we could leave it and he promised to keep an eye on it for us while we were gone. We put some raisins, chocolate, cheese and bread, from our boat box, in a small bag, then with that and our bedrolls under our arms we started walking across the highway bridge over the Mississippi River that tied Illinois to Missouri, the Show Me State, on the far side. It was a new bridge having been opened to traffic just five years before, in 1929. It had plenty of height in the center for steamboats to pass under easily without touching their stacks. From there we saw the *City of Helena* far down stream almost out of sight. As we came to the end of the bridge we put up our thumbs to approaching cars in hopes of hitching a ride toward the small town of Mansfield in Missouri. When I asked Erce about his home town, he said, "Mansfield is famous for being my birthplace, and not much else."

"Yeah, I know, but where is it?"

"It's southeast of Springfield, in the Ozark Mountains."

It took us two and a half days to make the 440 miles by many short rides. We slept in the woods at night. The people were all friendly and definitely not in a hurry. I remember one old fellow who gave us a ride in his ancient Model-T Ford through part of the mountains. The Ozarks are hills, ridges and valleys formed from a large plateau. We saw scrub oak on some of the hills and cedar growing in the valleys where streams meandered. When we came to the summit of a pass through the hills, he said, "This pass is the highest one in the Ozarks. I don't know if it's 2,000 feet or 20,000 feet high, but it is the highest."

Giving Erce a wink, I said, "2,000 feet is high enough for me. Let's not go any higher." Later I learned that the highest peak in the Missouri Ozarks, Taum Sauk Mountain, rises to only 1,772 feet, so the pass must have been somewhat less than that.

For the next week we visited with Ercell's grandfather Hart and five sets of uncles and aunts of his Shannon-clan side, scattered through the heart of the Ozarks. I met Bill, Walt, and Harry Shannon, and others I can't remember. We enjoyed every day of it, and how we did eat their good country cooking! We had chicken dinners four days in a row. I had never had gravy for breakfast before, but I found that it tasted good with hot biscuits and sausage. All their cooking was done on wood stoves—some were located outdoors where cooking was more comfortable in the summer time.

One day we went squirrel hunting—we didn't get any but had fun trying. Another day we tried horseback riding. Personally I liked riding in a canoe much better—because the horses were harder for me to control. Maybe if there had been a saddle on the horse and I had known how to ride better, I might have enjoyed it more. I went bumping along through forested, rolling hills where some of the rocky ground made me apprehensive of what might happen to me should I fall off. On the return trip I did make a "spectacular dismount" when my horse stopped suddenly and I went on over its head to meet the ground on my rear end. That ended my horseback riding. Erce rode better than I because he had long legs which he could clamp under the horse somewhat. Erce, after seeing that I wasn't hurt said, "Good show Pee Wee. You should join a circus."

Their farms were small—usually less than forty acres. They raised nearly all of their own food and didn't need much else, they told us. They seemed happy and satisfied with their way of life, living in log houses that probably had been built by their parents or grandparents, I thought, by the weathered look of the logs. Erce learned much about his genealogy from his elders and we were both treated royally by his family. After a week of good living we were running out of relatives to visit. There might have been a few cousins— "maybe moonshiners," I told Erce—that we missed, but not very many.

So once again we polished our thumbs and took to the road—this time eastward. We had better luck than the previous trip, making it to Poplar Bluff the first night and on back to Cairo the next morning. It had been a good break from our daily paddling, but we were anxious to be on our way to New Orleans, so we wrapped up our tired thumbs on the way to the warehouse where our canoe was stored. There we dumped our bedrolls, then went to town and found the U.S. Engineer's Office where we asked for charts of the river on to New Orleans.

A clerk said, "We don't give maps to just anyone—what boat are you on?"

"The *Islander*," we both stated at once.

"And what type of boat is the *Islander*?" he wanted to know.

"A seventeen-foot canoe," Erce informed him.

He looked up in surprise. After some more discussion he agreed that we truly could use the charts to help us find our way down the river, especially to locate some short-cuts through the shoots. He supplied us with a big, thick book of maps that rivermen use for navigating their steamers. Every detail of the channel was shown on them, including lights, buoys, depths of water, heights of bridges and markers on shore to steer by. The location of towns and the distances in miles between them was given, and that helped us in our record keeping—also we could plan ahead of time the places we might want to stop for water and supplies.

The river to Cairo had been fairly straight, but farther down there were bends that almost made circles. Shoots for small boats to use had been cut through some of the narrow necks of land between bends where the river doubled back on itself. We had some good and some bad experiences in them that I will relate as I get to them. The shoots were plainly shown on the maps, but not always easy to find on the river. In places the river looked like curls of hair or shavings from a plane on the charts. It appeared like we would make about as many—or maybe more—miles traveling east and west as we would going south, the direction we wanted to go.

Thumbing through the maps it seemed to us that the river's course looked like oxbow after oxbow most of the way to New Orleans.

After leaving the Engineer's Office with our book of maps we bought some food to stock our grub box, then launched our canoe from a small boat landing near the Ohio-Mississippi Rivers' confluence. A few people that had been watching us load up waved and wished us "good luck" as we settled into our usual positions and started paddling away.

The Ohio, about twice as big as the Mississippi at that point, was a milky color, a sharp contrast to the muddy water it joined. We headed across the river toward the Kentucky shore which we would skirt for awhile. The river had grown so big that to paddle down its middle was uninteresting, therefore we kept close to one bank or the other. Also the current was faster on the outside of the longer sweeping curves. We didn't save any time by cutting across from one point to another—in fact by doing so we often ran into a backwater where the current would be against us. We learned the hard way by trying to cross the river several times, but soon we just followed the river's current. When it crossed from one shore to the other, we went with it. Sometimes we saw small game, like a muskrat, or surprised some ducks by traveling close to the bank.

Below Cairo the width of the Mississippi River averages a mile wide at high water and somewhat less at other stages. Another reason for not being in the middle of the river was that if one of us had a hurried up call of nature and had to paddle a half mile to shore for relief, we might not make it in time. That never happened, but it could have.

While Erce paddled I read to him some information about the rivers from a booklet the engineers had given us: *Basic Data, Mississippi River, 1930*. "The depth of the water at Cairo can be as much as 87 feet and can drop to 30 feet at low water."

"Wow! A 57-foot drop—tell me more."

"The total length of the Missouri-Mississippi River to the Gulf of Mexico is about 4,200 miles, a distance 200 miles greater than either the Amazon or the Nile. The total length of the navigable waterway of the Mississippi River and its tributaries is estimated at 17,000 miles. The Mississippi starts at the outlet of Lake Itasca in northern Minnesota, and travels about 2,400 miles to the sea. The Ohio-Mississippi system is about the same length. There are fifty-four rivers flowing into the system that are navigable by steamboats, and many more smaller ones.

"The distance from Chicago to Grafton at the mouth of the Illinois River is 327 miles, from Grafton to Cairo at the mouth of the Ohio River is 233 miles, and from there to New Orleans is 969 miles for a total of 1,529 miles. The largest types of ships from all parts of the world visit the port of New Orleans, 108 miles from the Gulf of Mexico, and oil tankers proceed 132 miles farther upstream to Baton Rouge. The Mississippi drops 1,467 feet from Lake Itasca to the Gulf, and the current ranges from one to eight miles an hour."

"Let me know when we get to the eight mile an hour place, will ya? I think we're making one mile an hour now with you goofing off," Erce commented.

"I'm about done—let me finish," I went on. "Here's something interesting. The course of the river changes frequently, and landowners along the banks may be located in one state one day and in a different state the next due to a change in the river's course. During 1929, just before the Depression period, 61,000,000 tons of commerce was carried on the Mississippi River and its tributaries, mostly by powerful towboats which push strings of barges. The commodities transported included cotton, grain, sugar, coal, ore, oil, gasoline, steel products, cement, sand, gravel, and others—

all shipped at low cost." I continued, "On the Illinois River navigation is usually stopped by ice from December 1st to March 1st."

"It's a good thing we're off the Illinois, but I think the Mississippi may freeze up before you get to paddling again."

"I get the distinct impression that you would like me to paddle. I am just trying to educate you. Besides I think it must be about time to make camp, isn't it?"

I put the book away and picked up my paddle. Erce, of course, was just needling me for the fun of it. He was an easy going fellow with a good sense of humor and we often "poked fun" at each other to make light of most any situation.

Author holding the flag of the *Morton Downey*—1990

8

Cairo to New Orleans (968.8 Miles)

We didn't have much of the day left when we departed from Cairo, so paddled only eleven miles before making camp in Kentucky, the Bluegrass State, for the first and only time.

November 29th, Thanksgiving Day, dawned bright and clear, but by noon a strong wind started blowing and a cloud cover moved over us. Still, we had made about forty-five miles by evening, when we stopped at Donaldson Point Plantation to ask for some fresh water. We had only a one gallon jug for fresh water, therefore we had to stop almost daily someplace, usually a town, to fill it. We knew better than to use river water for anything other than washing, and sometimes we doubted the safety of that because we knew that not only did riverboats dump their sewage directly into the river but many towns did too, making the water unsanitary.

During the day we had crossed the river, so landed and pulled the canoe up on Missouri soil once more.

The weather looked pretty stormy as we walked the couple hundred yards from the river to the buildings which were old and unpainted. They looked temporary, sitting well up on blocks high enough that a large dog could run underneath without touching his ears. I guessed that early spring floods also ran under the house almost every year, because I could see water marks on the steps. We met a man sitting on the porch and asked for water. He pointed to a well nearby and said "help yourself." As Erce pumped the long iron handle, I held the jug at the pump spout until it filled. The man, who we assumed was the owner, asked, "Are you fellows camping out?"

"Yes, we have a canoe down by the river," I replied.

"It looks like a storm coming, so if you would like to stay in one of the empty cabins here, you're welcome." There were several cabins in a row extending out from the larger house.

"Thank you—" A ringing bell interrupted my words.

"That's a call to dinner, which you might as well come share with me," he continued.

"Thanks again—a true Thanksgiving," Erce happily accepted.

After washing and combing we went inside to find no one else around. I think the owner was in the kitchen telling the cook that there would be two more for dinner. There were benches at the two tables, and we picked one to sit down on, there being no chairs around. We should have stayed standing, because we had made the mistake of sitting down at the table where the black workers ate. When the black cook came in he got us up from there in a hurry and told us, "Sit at the white man's table," pointing to the other one. We learned that white and black definitely didn't mix at the table. Although the owner was alone, he had a separate table. It had been that way during slavery times and still was in many places in the Southland, we learned. Both races would have been embarrassed to mix. To change from the old ways was difficult.

While eating we learned about the large plantation of rich river-bottom land that sometimes flooded but was high and dry while we were there. Corn was the only crop, and the black men were doing the harvest work. After dinner, which was excellent—especially the cornbread—we went for our bedrolls and took the precaution of turning the canoe over and tying it down. We usually turned the canoe over at night, sometimes even sleeping under it when the weather looked threatening, but seldom tied it. During the night we were glad that we had because the wind howled and a heavy rain came with it. Before going to bed I wrote in our log, "This day I am thankful for the roof over us, a safe journey, and our good health."

Erce added, "and our good looks," his sense of humor showing up again. Perhaps our good health was partly due to our habit of eating large amounts of raisins—about fifty pounds during the trip. Erce once had a sore throat during his ricksha-pulling days, and that was the only time either of us felt unwell—that is if we overlooked tired feet and sea-sickness.

In the morning the wind continued to blow hard. The river had whitecaps showing on the tips of big waves. We needed to wait for better weather before continuing our cruise. We busied ourselves by sawing and splitting a big stack of firewood—thus getting in the good graces of the cook who had given us breakfast. I remember the afternoon especially well. We went to the field with the harvest crew to help pick corn. The owner called his men "darkies," which was a relatively polite name in those days. The term "blacks" hadn't come into use yet. In fact, I believe "black" might have been more offensive to them than "darkie" at that time.

"Negro" was used more than "black."

There were two wagons, each pulled by two mules. Two men walked behind a wagon husking the dried corn from the stocks and flipping the ears into the wagon—which had a high headboard to prevent the flying corn from going over the top. They picked corn from six rows at once. The wagon straddled two rows and there were two more rows on each side. The darkies would each quickly pick the ears from the outside rows and jointly pick the inside rows in a kind of race to see who could get to them first. The ears literally flew in a stream to the wagon. They didn't seem to be looking where they threw the ears, but they never missed. I tried to pick the two inside rows, but couldn't keep up and had to be helped. Then I would miss the wagon altogether sometimes. I was probably more trouble than I was worth, but we all had a good time that afternoon. Erce worked with the other crew and was having the same trouble that I had trying to keep up. Listening to the way the darkies sang and called to their mules was the most fun. In a way it was like they were singing a song.

"Move on dah, George! Hyeah me up dah? I'se talkin' to ya, mules."

"Wake up dah, Mable, Daddy gonna buy yo' new paha shoes."

"Ho! Whey deh!"

I suppose the tone of their voices, more than what they said, actually speeded up or slowed down the mules. Anyway, the mules responded by keeping just the right distance ahead of the pickers.

That evening we listened to old Uncle Sam, the caretaker, tell stories of how his Irish father had come to America and married a Mexican girl. That is what makes Americans, I thought—a mixture of all races.

December 1st the wind moderated some, so about seven —as the crew went to work—we started down the river again and left the harvesting of the corn crop to more able hands. We made only fourteen miles, to New Madrid, when the wind again drove us off the water for several hours. As we watched the river, a sailboat—about forty feet long and with her two masts tied together on deck—approached the landing but went on. We waved at the three people in the cockpit—one a pretty girl. As the boat's stern slid past we saw her name (the boat's—not the girl's), *Zarark of Chicago*. We had seen lots of barges and a few old river steamers, but that was the only sailboat we saw on the river. The masts had been taken down so that it could pass under the bridges safely.

Late in the afternoon we paddled about six more miles and camped. That night, even though we slept with our clothes on, the wind kept us cold all night. It seemed like winter had caught us and we still had a long way to go before we would be in a warmer climate. With the delays, we weren't making the daily runs we expected.

A heavy frost covered the ground in the morning and the wind still blew up the river. We struggled all day to make twenty-three miles. At night some River Folks, a man and his wife living in a shack just above the high water stage of the river, at a little place called Reelfoot, loaned us the use of an even smaller shack. Fortunately it had a bed we could spread our rolls on and a good roof above it. It rained during the night and we were thankful for the shelter.

The wind still blew hard in the morning and we knew it would be useless to try to paddle against it. We were about out of food, and there weren't any towns close on down the river, so we decided to walk the four miles inland to Ridgely for some provisions. Yes, we had crossed the river again and were on its eastern bank in the State of Tennessee, the Volunteer State.

In the afternoon, back at Reelfoot, to get out of the wind we wandered into an old church where we picked out tunes on a decrepit organ for several hours. Only a few people lived in the place, a cluster of cottages on the shore. They eked out a living by fishing and tending a garden in the summer. In the evening we listened to *Amos and Andy* on the "music box" with the River Folks—when the Old Lady wasn't talking about her doctor bills, her boat, gas engine, and everything else that concerned her. Andy and the King-fish were going at it as usual, on the radio, as were the Old Lady and her husband in real life—all at the same time. I couldn't tell which was more funny to listen to.

 After another night in the shack, we were anxious to get going. Even though the wind still blew, we prepared to leave. In five and a half days we had made only a hundred miles from Cairo, and at that rate it would be almost spring before we would get to New Orleans. The River People came out to see us off after we stopped at their place to thank them for the use of the shelter. The Old Lady said, "It'll cam."

"What's that?" I asked.

"The river, you know. It'll cam down."

"Oh yes," I said, finally figuring out what she was saying. She was right, too. The river did calm down in about an hour and we had a good day, making it to somewhere in Arkansas (the Land of Opportunity State) across on the western bank of the river. We had seen several flocks of ducks and geese—all heading south. Like us, they were getting tired of the bad weather. After supper we turned the canoe over the top of our grub-box, then took our bedrolls and headed for an old barn we had spotted from the river. It lay back from the river a hundred yards or so.

"Boy! Oh Boy! We're in luck," Erce said, looking into the barn.

"Yeah, man! Look at that hay." We slept warmly that night even though the weather outside was cold enough to freeze the eggs under a setting hen. That day finished our fifth month since we said farewell to our old home town of

Santa Monica. We had only twenty more shopping days until Christmas—which didn't bother us in the least—and only twenty more days to get to New Orleans before Christmas if we were to meet the goal we had set for ourselves when we left Chicago. December 5th was a beautiful day, cold but clear. We saw large flocks of ducks and great "swarms" of blackbirds that must have easily been several thousand birds. Their wings sounded like puffs of wind through the trees as they wheeled and turned together over our heads.

One of our problems on the canoe trip was finding fresh water. It seemed that all of the River People drank river water after the dirt settled. One old fellow we asked for water just pointed at the river and said, "That's good water—running water purifies itself in eighty feet, you know." Although that wasn't so, I couldn't argue with him, because he seemed to be doing all right drinking it. That night we boiled some water to fill our canteen for the next day. We had kept up a fairly steady stroke most of the day. After a good day's paddle of forty-three miles, helped along by the river's current, we had camped on Sunrise Towhead, an island on the Tennessee side of the channel.

In the morning we were up early and paddled forty-nine miles to Memphis, arriving about three. One doesn't notice the current while paddling in the river, but when coming alongside of a dock then you notice it and have to be careful. To be on the safe side when making a landing we would turn a half circle and paddle up stream to the dock, which is what we did at Memphis. We unloaded, pulled the canoe out and turned it over our things on dock. We never left the canoe in the water if we were going to be out of sight of it. At big towns we tried to find a private yacht club dock where we would ask permission to leave the canoe. We were never turned down.

The canoe secured, we walked uptown. Christmas decorations were everywhere—in store windows, on lamp posts,

Ercell on the *City of Helena*.

and hanging across the streets. People were busy shopping and hurrying about. We heard Christmas music in some of the stores and saw several Santas—some asking for money. We hadn't been to a large town since leaving Cairo and were in need of a shower, so we went to a YMCA where we cleaned up and had a swim. Afterwards, clean and full of joy, we walked around town some more, had our supper, then returned to the Memphis Yacht Club for the night. I slept in the Club dressing room and Erce slept in the cockpit of a Chris-Craft tied beside the dock next to our canoe.

We awakened to another frosty morning and paddled awhile before going ashore to cook our oatmeal for breakfast. It began to snow, lightly at first like scattered ashes falling down, then more heavily and driven along by the wind —which was with us for a change. The snow had held off until December 7th, but after a couple hours everything

ashore was blanketed with white. The river swallowed the
snow as it fell. We were anxious to get out of the snowy
country, so paddled hard all day and made a record run of
fifty-nine miles. Our southing wasn't that much because of
the river's looping course, but at least most of the snow on
shore had melted by the time we were ready to camp.

The next day we made it to Helena, Arkansas in time to
get our letters from home at the post office. That was always
a treat we looked forward to. Just to know everything was all
right with the folks at home made us feel good. We looked
up Captain Johnson and he told us we could stay aboard the
City of Helena for the night. He also pointed to his house and
said, "Go up there and make yourselves at home." We
bought some groceries, then went to his place to shave and
clean up for the good home-cooked supper Mrs. Johnson
provided. We were thankful for their warm welcome and
friendly hospitality. Later the folks went to town and left us

Ercell holding slab of ice, Mississippi River.

to listen to the radio until late in the evening when we retired to a warm cabin on their river steamer. It had been an enjoyable night—just like being at home. It might have made us a bit homesick, because it seemed like a long time since we had had such a relaxing evening.

We were up early, packed and started paddling, soon leaving Helena behind. We saw thousands of ducks and geese along the river every day and often wished we had a shotgun. Our mouths watered for a duck roasted over a campfire. The next few days were below freezing. The upturned roots of snags in the river were covered with ice. Everything wet or damp immediately froze stiff. Our slickers would stand by themselves. At night we put our water jug in a corner of our leaf mattress to keep it from being ice by morning. Our bottle of olive oil looked like white salve. December 11th we broke ice at water's edge to put the canoe in the river. Ice on the grass roots along the bank looked like crystal pendants on a chandelier. We slept with big piles of leaves under us and over us, but still had frigid feet before morning came. The next day we stayed in bed dreading the cold arising, but were surprised when we did get up that it had warmed up some over night and only a few icicles remained.

We bought grub in Arkansas City—which once had been a one-horse town, but only had a half-horse remaining. However the old store supplied us with what we needed and the old storekeeper even filled our water jug for us. He also told us a bit about the town. It was established about 1873 after the town of Napoleon at the mouth of the Arkansas River, about fifteen miles up the Mississippi, had been engulfed and the inhabitants were forced to seek other homes. "The only thing that keeps this town alive now is the County Courthouse," he said. There was a single row of business houses behind a high Mississippi levee, and they had been flooded many times. In 1927 one of the worst floods occurred

Frosty camp along the Mississippi River.

on the Mississippi. "Even though many miles of levees have been built to help control the flooding, some places still are flooded by water from the river occasionally."

We took our things and walked back to the river to try to make as much progress as possible before the day ended. Headwinds and a late start slowed us to only twenty-one miles for the day.

"Wow! Hot damn!" Erce said as he rolled out of bed on December 13th. "We're in the sunny Southland at last." It had warmed up considerably, to weather more like that of southern California.

We made better mileage that day, helped by a cut-off shoot between two oxbows. The shoot, so called because the current in it is faster than the river, is usually a dredged channel, but sometimes goes through an old river channel. They can be used only by small boats. We had fun with our canoe in the shoots, shouting as we shot along at ten to twelve miles per hour at times, but we had to watch the tricky currents very closely. Of course they saved us many miles of paddling, which made us happy. If the current wasn't very strong at the entrance of the shoot, then the channel might be blocked part way through, and it was usually better to follow the river. On one occasion we got about one and a half miles through a shoot and had to return to the river because the channel dried up. Not counting the extra three miles, we still made fifty-nine miles (as the river flowed) before camping on Howard Island—which was really an island only during high water when the river entered an old channel to separate the island from the shore.

We started off the following day by going through Worthington Point cut-off, thus saving six miles of paddling. In the early afternoon we got our long-hoped-for opportunity of catching a wounded duck that had been unable to fly away with its flock. There were many hunters along the shores and we knew that not all ducks shot were retrieved. We had often talked about what we would do if we saw one. The duck we found couldn't fly, but it surely could dive under water when we got close to it. When it did, we had to wait for it to come up before we could go after it again. After an hour's chase, mostly paddling in circles and wondering where the duck would emerge next, the unlucky ducky was captured and made the supreme sacrifice for our benefit. I almost fell in the river once when I grabbed for the duck and missed.

Shortly after our duck hunt a USED boat came along and we were offered a tow to Lake Providence, Louisiana (the Pelican State) a few miles away. We accepted. Arriving there, the engineer gave us a ride in his car uptown, where we bought some groceries. It seemed strange to ride in a car after so many months of not having done so. Returning to the canoe, we started on, passing Stack Island which had formed around a sunken Standard Oil barge. Before dark we camped and prepared a delicious dinner of boiled duck with noodles, baked potatoes, and toast. We were well rewarded for our persistence in the duck hunt. We slept in Louisiana for the first time and were forty-nine miles closer to New Orleans than we were the night before. Also we were a little past halfway from Cairo to that city, which meant we still had about 450 miles to travel. The weather had been better and we were enjoying that.

The next morning we passed Atherton Towhead, which made us think of home and our good friend, Ray Atherton, another member of our Sea Scout group. We decided we would have to tell him about "his" Towhead on the Mississippi. We had an exciting ride going through Willow Point cut-off where there were many whirlpools, eddies and boils. That shoot saved us ten miles, so it was worth it, but at times I wondered if we would make it through without swamping— we knew not what lay ahead. The banks were about forty feet apart and very steep, so we couldn't stop or turn around. The current was too fast for that anyway. Once we started we were committed to go all the way through. I can still hear Ercell yell, "Pull, Pee Wee—*Pull!*" Even though the shoot was only a few miles long, I never expected to run into excitement like that on the "slow and lazy" Mississippi River. Once back in the main river we breathed more easily and were slowed down to the usual two to three miles per hour.

Not many more miles of paddling brought us to Vicksburg, Mississippi (the Magnolia State). We stopped there to check out the old Civil War battlefield that we had heard about, but we found it more interesting walking in town eyeing the many southern beauties doing their Christmas shopping. Rather than looking at cold statues in a park, real live people were more appealing to us. Vicksburg was dressed up for the holidays with bright lights and Christmas trees along the main street.

We didn't stay long in Vicksburg, or any other town, but kept going. We paddled under the Mississippi River bridge

N
25

there—being careful to keep away from the piers where the current could cause a canoe to tip over. We went on until almost dark, making fifty-five miles. Seeing a good beach, we pulled in near some fishermen's shanty-boats and camped. One of the fishermen came to our campfire and yarned with us awhile. I never learned his name, but remember him for his extremely bushy eyebrows. I was interested in his way of life, so asked him, "Do you make a living by fishing?"

"I get along by trading fish for vegetables with the 'niggers'," he said.

"Are there many of them around here?" I questioned.

"Yes, more of them than us," he said, as though he wasn't too happy about that.

After we answered a couple of his questions about our canoe trip, he told us a story about the fickleness of the old Mississippi and the cleverness of a small boy. He said, "The Yazoo River, coming in from the northeast now runs along the waterfront at Vicksburg, but it wasn't always that way— the Mississippi once did. When the Mississippi changed channels in 1876 it left the town high and dry. The townspeople didn't know what to do, but knew the town would die if it wasn't a river port. A small boy suggested to the engineers that the Yazoo could be diverted to take the Mississippi's place at Vicksburg's waterfront. They thought it over and found the idea to be very practical. They built a dam at the mouth of the Yazoo and when it was closed, the waters flowed—just like the boy predicted—in front of the town, giving it a water course again and a happy town."

We also learned that across from the town was an island named after DeSoto, the explorer who is given credit for discovering the Mississippi River in May of 1541. He died a year later and was buried in the waters that would give his name immortality. As our campfire died down, we said "good night" to the fisherman-historian and turned to the job of making our beds for the night.

We had a good day on December 16th for two reasons. The first was that we arrived at a USED Q-boat just in time to be invited to Sunday dinner. We came alongside their boat and asked for fresh water. After a little conversation with the men, the boss said, "Why not tie your canoe up and come aboard to have dinner with us?"

"That sounds great to us—thanks," I replied, already tying the canoe to a post. (What a sneaky way to get a free meal—but it usually worked.)

Those workers ate even better than people in the CCC camps we had visited. We had chicken, dressing, peas, macaroni with cheese, mashed potatoes, corn bread, pineapple and grated cheese salad, ice cream, cake, and coffee. What a feast the black cook and mess boys gave us. Just thinking about that good food made for happy paddling the rest of the day. The other nice thing that happened was that by taking Diamond Point cut-off we made sixty-five miles that day—a new record. To top the day off, we watched a gorgeous, vividly-colored sunset from our camp.

MISSISSIPPI RIVER

It was a good thing we enjoyed that day because the following day was altogether different. It rained from early morning for the rest of the day, with thick, dripping fog over the river. We crept along close to the bank to keep from losing our way. We were soaked as we passed Waterproof, Louisiana. What a name! We missed the cut-off there, but made the next one at Giles Bend. The left bank, the Mississippi side, was high, almost a hill, something we hadn't seen for days. Some days we would see nothing higher than the levee or maybe some cottonwood trees.

Much of the country in back of the levee was low river bottom land. The fog lifted as we approached the town of Natchez, where we were expecting and received some mail. That was the one bright star in that otherwise gloomy day. When we got back to our canoe the rain hadn't lessened any and we didn't want to go on, so we looked around for a shelter. A ferryboat tied in a slip didn't look like it was going anywhere, so we asked a watchman if we could stay on board. "Sure, come in and dry out by my fire," he said. We spent the night on the ferry, which was very comfortable and surely a stroke of good luck for us.

It rained some the next day again, but not as much. We had to pass by Glasscock Point cut-off because it was dry in the middle. We had started in but hadn't gone very far when a fisherman we came upon told us, "You can't get all the way through, boys." So we went back to the river and around the long way.

Some of the names of places revealed on our charts were interesting, but we could only guess at how they came about. We came to Dead Man's Bend and thought a dead man may have been found there. We passed it safely and shortly afterwards camped on the Louisiana shore. Mississippi was still on the other side of the river. We found a nice place near some trees where we could get wood for a fire and leaves for a bed. In the evening we looked at our charts by the light of our campfire and candle light to figure the miles on to New Orleans.

"How many miles to go?" I asked.

"About 215, which means four or five days more."

"Tomorrow is the 19th, so we can still make it by Christmas—right?"

"I don't see any more cut-offs, but still we should make it if the weather holds good. By the way, what are you going to get me for Christmas?" Erce asked.

"A silver-new-nothing to wear on your thumb—good night, Erce."

The following day after paddling for several hours we stopped at an old deserted plantation, where a faded American flag still waved in the breeze. The well pump worked, after we primed it, so we filled our water jug and ate lunch as we explored around. There wasn't anything left there worth much. We went on until evening when we stopped for grub at the little town of Phillipston at the mouth of the Lower Old River, formed by the Red River and the Atchafalaya River. From there, for the rest of the way, we were totally in Louisiana. After supper we decided to paddle awhile in the quiet and peace of a calm evening twilight. We went on until about eleven-thirty with the nearly full moon providing light for us. It was a beautiful night and one of the pleasant memories I have of the trip.

Baton Rouge, capital of Louisiana, was next on our list of places to stop. The following day, while still about twenty miles away (by river), we sighted the tower of the thirty-two story capitol building. It had been built by Huey Long, the governor (1928–1931) known as the "Kingfish" who ruled his state with an iron hand and armed guards, dictator style. He even ruled the governor that followed him until Huey was assassinated in the capitol building (1935) by Dr. Weiss, a political enemy. His nickname came from his slogan, "Every Man A King." It grew dark before we got there, but we could see the capitol because it was lighted by various colored lights—a striking landmark.

The old yellow moon rose slowly from the river directly ahead of us as we paddled quietly along its golden path. The reflections on the water, distorted by the wind-made ripples, looked like a golden stairway leading to the base of a black marble pillar with the moon a golden globe atop it. The moon put the capitol building lighting to shame.

We arrived at the waterfront, found a place to secure the canoe, then went to town and had a refreshing shower at the "Y." Afterwards we walked around town and viewed the capitol by moonlight. Getting tired, we went back to the dimly lit boat landing, where I slept in the canoe, while Erce found a ferryboat to stay in. The weather had turned balmy, quite a contrast to only a few days before when we had snow and winter conditions. We were happy about that and slept warm for a change.

Ken and Erce in Islander arriving in New Orleans.

The country below Baton Rouge was low and swampy back of the levee. Many little burgs along the river disclosed their location by house tops and church steeples only. We even saw a few palm trees, which made us think of our home in California. To gain some extra miles, we paddled in the moonlight again and in the warmer weather were bothered some by mosquitoes. The air was so warm we could hardly believe that it was almost Christmas.

Voices and sounds carried clearly for a long distance over the water. We could hear the children shouting to each other from a long way off. At one place the syncopated notes of a trumpet and strains from a fiddle were playing "Darkness on the Delta," followed by "The Peanut Vendor" and then "Stormy Weather." We enjoyed their music for several miles and "knew" they were playing especially for us. We softly sang the words along with the music, but I don't suppose they heard us.

MISSISSIPPI RIVER 1934.

Sunday, December 23rd, we started from Forty-Eight-Mile-Point (miles up river from New Orleans) in the morning and camped at dusk two miles below the town of Kenner and about sixteen miles from New Orleans. That night we had our last campfire on the "Ol' Mississippi," and we sat a long while talking more than usual. We looked back on the trip and decided that even though it was cold at times, it had been a good one, worthwhile, and we had enjoyed it. We had learned much about the country and its people and seen lots of sights we might never see again—but what we should do on the morrow when we got to New Orleans was very much on our minds.

"Well Buddy, it looks like, with only sixteen miles to go, we are going to get to that 'Mystical City' before Christmas," I said.

"I don't think anything, short of a tornado, can stop us now."

"What are we going to do, besides enjoy the Yuletide, when we get there?" I asked.

"I've been thinking about that. Let's go over our options," Erce very logically said.

We thought some of canoeing the Intra-coastal Waterways System along the coast to and in Florida, but figured there might be too much open sea for a canoe. Besides we might have been tiring of canoeing just a bit. We thought of starting to hitch-hike home, but not very enthusiastically. Our third choice was to sell the canoe, since we needed money again, then try to ship out on a freighter as seamen. We both had some experience on small boats, but not on ships. Finally we decided we should try to get a job on a ship and maybe we could go to a foreign country, now that we had "conquered" America. "Why not give it a try?" we reasoned, and we shook hands.

We had been together for nearly six months, under trying conditions at times. There were nights when we slept on the bare hard ground, times when we had been hungry, cold and miserable, still during all that time we never had a break in our friendly relationship. I know that I couldn't have had a better buddy than Erce.

TRUE LOVE

A man and his canoe are one together,
A true love that will last forever.
With lines so graceful, a smooth shapely form,
Like a maiden once held, so lovely and warm.

A canoe glides along, like a leaf in a breeze,
Silent and peaceful, you paddle with ease.
Time's of little importance, and as you float,
Trouble and worry seem strangely remote.

We think of the Voyageurs, canoemen of the past,
And the trails they followed, in a country so vast.
To be courageous like them, is our desire,
To challenge the rapids, like those we admire.

The Voyageurs' songs, we hear in the wind,
Around a campfire, like strains from a violin.
We gather together to sing with great joy,
Of the oneness and freedom none can destroy.

When an old canoeman dies, he keeps paddling along,
To a Heaven called Grand Portage, where good men
    belong.
He will dance to the fiddles, in the Great Hall[1],
Greet old friends, feast, and forever stand tall.

—KEN WISE
December 18, 1989

---

[1]The main building of the Northwest Company at Grand Portage.

Part Three

Ordinary Seamen
Thousands of miles by slow freighter

As an ordinary seaman, I served my time,
First on the *Oritani*, then on the Point line.
Winter in the Atlantic, how we did roll,
To be on land again, was my only goal.

The decks were icy, I could not stand,
On the seat of my pants, I once did land.
Docked at Philadelphia, I was real glad,
To leave the ship, didn't make me sad.

But in one week, I was ready to go,
Down the Delaware River, facing some snow,
Into New Orleans, we went once more,
Left the *Oritani*, glad for the shore.

On the *Point Palmas*, I liked it much better,
I even had time, to write a long letter.
Through the Panama Canal, into the Pacific,
The ocean was calm, the weather terrific.

Made Los Angeles harbor, before we were due,
On to San Francisco, where I was through.
I hitch-hiked home, in the warm sun,
End of my story, that's all, it's done.

9

New Orleans to Philadelphia

It didn't take us long to paddle on to New Orleans, Louisiana's chief city, the next morning.

"Yeah boy!" This is the sunny Southland of cotton and sugarcane, Creole and Cajun," Erce said.

"Man! Look at all those ships," I countered, pointing across the river opposite the city. There were about seventy-five old freighters, tied together in rows of six or more, rusting away in disuse. Either our shipping business had gone to pot or else the ships had been used in wartime and were no longer needed. We suspected the latter. Along the city docks we saw several ships, loading or unloading freight, flying foreign flags. Maybe we would be aboard one of them when it started down the river headed for some strange port, we imagined. We spotted a USED Q-boat and tied alongside to ask permission to store the canoe on deck while we went ashore to look around. The boss-man greeted us warmly, especially after he heard that we had paddled all the way from Chicago, and said, "Make yourselves at home here until you get established elsewhere." He told us we could eat and sleep aboard the Q-boat.

"Thank you. That's very friendly of you," Erce said. "Would you mind taking our picture?" I asked as I dug into my pack for my seldom-used Kodak. That was how we celebrated our arrival at New Orleans.

We loitered along the waterfront looking at the ships. Some bananas, or maybe plantains, a larger variety of the same family, were coming out of the hold of one ship and being carried ashore by workers. We walked through a picturesque old section of town, which we later learned was the French Quarter, on our way to the main post office. There we received with joyous hearts our expected Christmas mail. There were even some packages for us which helped us survive our first Christmas away from home. We took everything back to the Q-boat where we could open and enjoy their contents. What did I get? Socks, of course—well, I needed them. We did get cookies, too.

After having supper with the small crew aboard, we spent a leisurely evening writing letters to let our folks at home know we had arrived safely. From their letters we could tell they were anxious about us, because we hadn't written to them very often while on the river trip. We spent the rest of the evening listening to Christmas music on the radio. In 1934 radio was fairly new and still somewhat of a novelty to us. We were happy to have arrived at our destination before Christmas, a day not meant to be spent alone on a river bank anywhere.

After a hearty breakfast on the Q-boat and wishing those aboard and each other a "Merry Christmas," Erce and I slid the canoe back into the river, loaded up, and paddled to the Industrial Canal where there were more ships. It was a connecting link between the river and Lake Pontchartrain, a large lake east of the city, where the Southern Yacht Club had their docks and moorages. We were heading there in hopes of finding a sale for our canoe. Part way through the canal we came to a ship lock that we didn't know about. The operator said, "No Christmas present today, boys. Cough up a dollar or you don't go through." Our finances were very low again, so we portaged the canoe, which weighed about ninety pounds, around, then went back for our gear. We carried everything in one more load and thus saved ourselves an easy buck.

We reached the lake and yacht club in the afternoon. The lake looked like a fine place for sailing. Much to our surprise we spotted the *Zarark of Chicago* at one of the moorings and paddled alongside to greet the owners who were on deck. We recalled seeing its pretty passenger when it passed us one windy day about three weeks before.

"Hello there, voyageurs. I remember passing you on the river," Mr. Zimmerman, the owner, said. "Come aboard."

"Thanks. We remember you, too," I told him. "Back at New Madrid."

He introduced us to his wife and daughter, whom he embarrassed by saying, "Jean, sweet sixteen." I must have thought she was sweet, too, because when we were alone later, Erce wanted to know if I was "lovesick, homesick, or seasick?" I guess I had been rather quiet and a bit bashful around Jean. Anyway I continued being quiet by not answering him. They had invited us back and were all very nice to us when we came to have a wonderful Christmas dinner with them on their yacht.

Finally I found my tongue and said, "It's a real treat for us to have dinner with you. We feel real honored."

"We're glad to share and pleased to have company," Mrs. Zimmerman remarked. "We would have been alone too, if you hadn't come along." Jean was quiet too, probably as bashful as I.

After the baked ham dinner with all of the trimmings, we stayed aboard to visit awhile with the interesting family. They had traveled extensively and had their boat fixed up very comfortably. That's the way to go if one can afford it. We enjoyed that warm, beautiful Christmas night with the Zimmermans. For our own accommodations, we found a cruiser in a boathouse where no one would notice us, tied the canoe alongside, and bedded in its spacious cockpit.

In the morning we went to the yacht club, where we left our gear, then canoed to town down a different canal. We went to the Boy Scout headquarters, steamship offices, and freight companies trying to get a lead on freighter jobs. We had no real luck that first day. At the "Y" a newspaper reporter and photographer got our story and took our picture for the paper—which gave us a good advertisement for selling the canoe and indicated our desire to get jobs on a freighter. In fact, the next day a man came to see us at the yacht club and offered us thirty dollars for the *Islander*. As that was five dollars more than we paid for it in Chicago, we accepted. Our faithful canoe had served us well without any trouble at all. Parting with it was like saying goodbye to a friend. We helped the buyer load the canoe onto his truck.

"Take good care of her, will you?" I asked.

"Sure will. Don't worry," and he waved good-bye. We waved good-bye—more to the canoe than to him.

That evening Erce went to a Sea Scout meeting and spent some time with the members while finishing his Able Sea Scout badge. Able is next to the highest rank in Sea Scouting. Erce had started the work for the badge before leaving home. He passed with "flying colors." When he got back to the yacht club where I had been listening to a radio, we wandered back to the cruiser for another night's sleep.

The second day in town we had better luck. We met Mr. Rice, a ship's captain who told us a ship named *Oritani* was taking on a new crew. "Go see its chief mate," he said. We were told that the ship was at the Todd Shipyard in Algiers across the river. We walked miles in the rain to get there just to be told to come back at eight in the morning. That night we had to pick a different cruiser to sleep on, because the owner was aboard our regular one.

December 28th we were up at 5:00 AM in order to get to the Todd Shipyard by eight. It was worth it, because the Mate signed us on as Ordinary Seamen (O.S.). The boatswain showed us where we could bunk in the forecastle and then put us to work. That was quick, and we considered ourselves fortunate. In two days we had found a ship and on the third morning were at work. We were at the right spot at the right time, helped by a good informant. I know there were hundreds of men looking for work—although some seamen may not have wanted to sign on the *Oritani* of New York because she was a small ship, as freighters go, and because of her destination to the cold country along the Atlantic seaboard. Why leave a warm place like New Orleans and maybe be stuck in some cold place? Erce and I were not experienced enough to know those things. We didn't realize the *Oritani* was small or even know where she was headed. We had a job and that was all that concerned us. The seamen's union wasn't strong at that time—at least not in New Orleans—or else we probably wouldn't have been hired. In some ports all the hiring was done through the seamen's union office where you waited your turn for a job.

Our first job was to pull in the shore lines as we moved ship to the loading dock where we put the lines out again. Black stevedores loaded the holds with paper and other freight for Tampa and Philadelphia. It was interesting to watch the men work and listen to their talk. They happily joked with one another. At noon I went ashore with one of the other seamen to an eating place because our ship's galley wasn't set up yet. I told him before going inside the small cafe on the waterfront, "I should clean up first."

He said, "Don't do that. Stay dirty, it shows people you have a job and you can be proud of that."

In the afternoon "Boats" (short for Boatswain Mate) gave us ship's leave to go get our personal gear. We hurried around to collect the final payment for our canoe, go get and mail our sleeping bags home, and get back aboard with our extra clothes by four o'clock—at which time I went on watch. Erce wasn't due to go on until midnight, so went to his bunk for some rest. My watch was for eight hours and then I had sixteen hours off. As Erce came on watch, I got off.

We just had to keep our eyes on the gangway and ship in general—like checking the shore lines and "rat guards" on the shore lines, metal discs about sixteen inches wide that fit over the rope hawser to prevent rats and mice from coming up the line to the ship. Our duties also included anything the watch officer might want us to do. The three other Ablebody Seamen (A.B.) took over during the day time. These were men who had been to sea before, had experience aboard ship, and served their apprenticeship as Ordinary Seamen.

The deck force on the *Oritani* consisted of the three A.B.'s, we two O.S.'s and the bos'n—really a small crew, especially at sea, we were to find out later. The captain, first, second, and third mates were the officers. A black cook and a couple of Filipino mess boys were the galley crew. Then the engineers were made up of three officers and three crew men. They were called "the black-gang"—although none of them were black.

Our quarters were fairly good, with two men to a cabin with upper and lower bunks—no doors. A washroom was shared by the six men on the deck force. The black-gang had quarters elsewhere, as did the galley crew. Our boss was the bos'n and I liked him really well—maybe because he was small like me and, unlike the officers, friendly. He let me go ashore in the morning to mail some letters and make a last call to the post office to check for mail.

By noon the ship, loaded and the lines taken in, started down the river. I saw the action because I wasn't on watch and enjoyed the anticipation of seeing more of the river and the delta area below New Orleans, which extended over one hundred miles into the Gulf of Mexico. When I went on watch at four the fog had started to roll in. I stood in the peak of the bow as a lookout to shout to the officer on the bridge anything I saw ahead. The ship had been slowed down to just steerage-way speed. When the fog got so thick we couldn't see a half-ship's length ahead, the "hook" (anchor) was "dropped" (lowered) and the ship swung around on the current, its head back upstream as the anchor took hold. For the rest of my watch I rang a bell every few minutes to warn any advancing ship that we were at anchor. That was a monotonous but important job. At midnight Erce took over my duty and I sacked in, but sleep didn't come easily because the ringing bell was just above me.

It took us all the next day to reach the Gulf, and a day and a half to make it on to Tampa. Beyond the end of the river we followed a line of buoys until reaching deep water all around. The weather was warm, the Gulf fairly calm. Land soon disappeared from sight—we were at sea. By standing night watch, I had, when not sleeping, the day free to watch the ocean and shore—when we were close enough. We approached Tampa at night when I was on lookout watch. I could see the glow of the city lights long before I saw the lights marking the ship channel entrance. I reported to the bridge at once, "lights dead ahead, sir."

"Very well" was what I heard back from the bridge.

The ship had just been tied to the wharf when the New Year blew in—and how it blew, with every whistle in town and on the ships in port blasting forth. Erce rang eight-bells (twelve o'clock) and the mate pulled on the ship's whistle cord. We were right in the spirit of the celebration at the start of 1935. The black stevedores started unloading our freight without any delay. The next morning Erce and I got together for a short stroll ashore—so as to be able to say we had been in Florida—then had a good turkey dinner aboard ship at noon for New Year's.

At sundown the *Oritani* cleared the harbor for the trip around Florida to the Atlantic Ocean. The days were warm and the sea calm as we rounded Key West, at about 23° north latitude, our farthest point south. One of my duties on watch was lookout, sometimes on the bow and other times on the bridge, where I had to bring coffee to the officer in charge when he wanted it. Also I would call the next watch in time to get ready to relieve us. On the bow I would repeat the bells that I heard from the bridge, I think mainly for the officer to know that his lookout hadn't fallen asleep.

I didn't get to steer the ship—the A.B.'s did that, on a four on, eight off basis. On January 3rd, about noon, we could see Miami as we passed along close to shore. We made the hatches water tight by covering them with boards, then canvas—"batten down the hatches." We stowed shore lines away below deck, lashed down other things on deck that might wash about, and the hawsehole where the anchor chain ran through we filled with concrete to keep water from washing up on deck—sometimes a wooden block was used instead of concrete. The ship was prepared for rough weather—in sailor terms, made "shipshape," and none too soon, because the sea was "kicking up."

The next day the wind grew strong and the sea rough. When not on watch, Erce and I stayed in our bunks afraid to get up to eat for fear we would lose anything we ate to the fish. Our watches were increased to nine hours—mine from 7:00 PM to midnight and from 8:00 AM to noon. Erce had midnight to 5:00 or 6:00 AM and from 1:00 to 4:00 or 5:00 PM. Our daytime duty was to wash the white paint—aboard ship we called it "sugeeing."

The wind blowing directly against the Gulf current made the sea very rough as we headed into the wind. The bow of the ship would nose under a wave, pick up tons of water, and wash the deck with it. We had to be careful going from the forecastle to mid-deck not to get washed away. We strung a line between them to hang on to. That night I had to be called twice before I got up nerve enough to get up for watch. Once I got to the bridge where I stood watch I felt better than I did in the foul air of the forecastle where the men were smoking. I was eating sometimes and heaving part of the time. My stomach surely didn't have its "sea-legs."

Six days out of Tampa we sighted land and soon headed up the Delaware River, with that state on our port side and New Jersey on the starboard. The third mate was skippering and I, serving as lookout on the bow, called out the lights on the buoys as they came in view. Cakes of ice floated down the river and the weather was freezing cold, but not as bad as at sea where the wind made it colder. At midnight we arrived in Philadelphia. After tying the ship up, at which all hands worked, I gladly flopped in my bunk. Erce went on watch.

"Take over, Buddy. We just came up the Delaware River," I said.

"Good show, Pee Wee. I'll watch things while you sleep," Erce said as he went on deck. We were always trading places, so we didn't see much of each other. He did tell me that we were scheduled to start back to New Orleans the next day.

After a few hours' sleep I got up and had some breakfast. Since I wasn't on watch, I strolled to town, walking through an interesting foreign part where people spoke a language I didn't understand. Philly appeared to be an old colonial town with narrow streets and no spaces between houses. I went to a theatre and saw the show, *Happiness Ahead*, with the song, "Pop Goes Your Heart." Then I went to the "Y" for a swim—just like always when Erce and I got to town, but this time I was alone. I had been paid $12.82, at the rate of $35.00 per month, for eleven days' work. That was the first money I had earned in six months and I was happy to have some money in my pocket for a change. In port I was assigned to night watch, which was increased to ten hours—from ten PM to eight AM. There wasn't much to do, so I spend most of my time in the galley, where it was warm, eating and reading *Plum Pudding* by Christopher Morley.

At noon I found out that actually the *Oritani* wasn't going to New Orleans—she wasn't going anywhere. They were going to tie her up because of a slowdown in shipping—they had no freight for her. The entire crew would be laid off. Ercell had gotten a job on another Moore McCormack ship and had asked for a job for me—but when I got to the mate he had already hired someone else. Erce had been at the right spot at the right time while I was on my "sleep watch." Perhaps there were other reasons I didn't get on—like being too small or getting seasick. Maybe the mates had talked about who was best to hire—and I wasn't the best—so after six months together Erce and I planned our separate trails.

We had sad hearts, but who knows, maybe it was for the best. A little independence probably did us both good. In the process of growing up we each have to stand alone at times. We had gone a long way together, but Erce had a right to do as he wished. His ship, the *Commercial Quaker* of New York, would be going to South America, something we both wanted to do. I was glad that he had the chance to go, even if I didn't.

Erce was standing night watch aboard his ship, while I was doing the same on the *Oritani*. They were tied alongside of each other. We had midnight lunch together in the galley of the *Commercial Quaker*. We called it the "galley watch" because that is where we spent most of our time in the early morning hours with nothing to do in between making our rounds of the ships every hour or so. We wrote letters and talked and talked. We hadn't done much of that on the trip because of different watch times—so we made up for it that one night. Some of our conversation went like—

"Do you know where you'll be going in South America?

"Just down the East Coast, I think."

"Send me a post card from every port you go to, will you?"

"Sure, but where to?"

"Well, here or maybe New Orleans if the *Oritani* sails again."

"You going to be a sailor?" Erce asked.

"No way! You know better than that. How about you?"

"Me? No, I just want to travel a bit."

Little did we know then that we both would be sailors during World War II. Ercell would become a Navy pilot and I a deck officer on a Coast Guard ship not much bigger than the *Oritani*. When our watch ended we said, "See you later." Actually it turned out to be *much* later, and back in Santa Monica after three months had gone by.

I got four hours' sleep, and as I was called up, the *Oritani* was pulling away from the *Commercial Quaker*. Getting on deck, I looked for Erce, but he was nowhere in sight. It was best that way, because I am sure I would have broken down after a hug. I silently said, "Good-bye, buddy," but there wasn't time for weeping.

We went down the Delaware River to the Sun Shipyards at Chester, Pennsylvania (south of Philly), anchoring for a half hour once on the way because of fog. I didn't have to stand night watch there, so I had a good night's sleep for a change. The crew worked all day stowing equipment, washing down decks and putting out steel cables for shore lines. The weather had warmed up above freezing, which helped make the work more pleasant. The *Commercial Quaker* with Erce aboard left port that day although I didn't see her go. I got $4.00 more pay, had my last meal aboard that night, and was discharged—but Boats let me sleep aboard.

In the morning I left ship, sad in some respects but glad in others. Sad because I didn't have a job any more and glad because I was leaving a somewhat miserable job—especially when seasick. I made my way back to the "Y" in Philly. I had told the mate that would be my address in case the *Oritani* did sail again and he wanted me—which I doubted, although he did give me a very good discharge signed by the captain.

Thinking that I might be in Philly a long time and I would have to conserve my meager pay, I asked the clerk at the "Y" if he knew of a cheaper place where I could stay. "Maybe I do," he said. "Wait a minute." He picked up the phone and made a call—after which he handed me a piece of paper with an address on it and said, "Go there and tell them I sent you."

I found the place all right, but didn't know if I had been given the right address. The building was a nice looking home in a residential area. I had expected something like the transient building in Chicago. I knocked on the door and was greeted by a cheery young man, Mr. Wrighter, who asked, "Are you the fellow from the 'Y'?"

"Yes, I am." After introductions, he showed me around the house, then assigned me a room with two nice beds in it on the second floor. "I probably can't afford this," I said.

"It won't cost you anything, and the meals are free, too," he said smiling.

"I can't quite believe that," I said in wonderment.

"This is a co-op. Everyone here helps with the work of cleaning and cooking when their turn comes up—so if you are willing to do that, you can stay."

"Sure, of course I'll do my part."

"Okay, make yourself at home," he said, gave me another smile and left. I did as he said, walked around and looked the place over again. The old home called the "Season House" had gas lamps on the walls. In the large living-room, where several fellows were lounging, a gas flame glowed in a large fireplace. I met some of the other occupants who were all friendly. Most of them I learned were from Philly. I still couldn't quite believe my good fortune of finding a place that didn't cost anything except some work. It was warm, comfortable, and clean—for the time being my needs were taken care of.

Later when I talked to my roommate about the place, he said, "It's owned by a rich man with a big heart and operated for down—but not out—white-collared young men looking for jobs. I think 'Mr. Smiles' who runs the place is a 'fairy' because he's always going around pinching people. Watch out for him." There were about twenty-five young fellows living in the house, which was run a little like a fraternity—dormitory style. We had oatmeal with milk for breakfast and beans and bread for supper. It wasn't fancy, but "for the price" I thought it was darn good food. For lunch we were on our own, but not at the home.

The next day after breakfast, feeling free, I visited what I thought was the most important place to see in Philadelphia, Independence Hall where the Liberty Bell was housed. The building was the place where in 1776 the Declaration of Independence was adopted. Built in 1732, a tower was added in 1750 for the Liberty Bell shipped from England that year. It was formally opened as a National Museum on July 4, 1876 after one hundred years of independence. I read the inscription on the very large bell, "Proclaim Liberty throughout all the land unto all the inhabitants thereof." It was rung every July 4th until 1835 when it cracked. After that it became a museum relic. I never would have seen the Hall or Bell had I not lost my ship and been put ashore. Erce didn't have time to get ashore much before he left for South America, so maybe I was the lucky one after all.

From the Hall I went to the Delaware River bridge where I walked to its middle for a good view of Camden,

New Jersey on one side and Philadelphia on the other. It was city as far as I could see. Later at the post office I received a couple of letters from home. That made me think about how I was three thousand miles away from that home and I couldn't help but wonder how I was going to get back. Although that bothered me some, I was determined to make the best of the situation by seeing what I could of Philly. Sunday I enjoyed church with some of the other fellows from the house, then spent some time at my newly-found home in the afternoon reading—*Out of the Silent North* by Harry Sinclair.

We had better meals on Sunday, but still only two. Monday I was put on house duty—cleaning floors and washing dishes, which didn't take very long because I had help. The Board of Directors met in the morning and we house members had a meeting in the afternoon. We voted to have a dance party and planned it for Wednesday night. Mr. Wrighter approved it. Things were getting better all the time, except that I didn't have any good clothes to wear. That problem was unexpectedly solved for me the next day.

Tuesday was really hectic. In the afternoon I wandered down to the Moore McCormack wharf, thinking that I should keep in touch with the job market, and to my surprise, the *Oritani* was tied alongside. I went aboard and talked to the chief mate about getting my job back. "Sure," he said. "I tried to get in touch with you at the "Y," but you weren't there. Go see the boatswain."

Because of his surprised look, I thought maybe he actually had tried, and then again maybe he hadn't—but it little mattered. Boats put me right to work, because as before he was short-handed. The ship moved out into the river and I was worried that I didn't have my things from the Seasons House. I was glad when we tied up again on the Camden side to load some freight, then moved back across the river to the original spot. When we had a breathing spell, I told Boats, "I don't have any clothes aboard." He told me to hurry and get my gear, because they were leaving very soon. I ran ashore to get a taxi to take me to the home which was half way across town. Luckily I did flag one down quickly and jumping in, said to the driver, "2204 Walnut Avenue, and hurry."

"Right, Boss."

Getting to the house, I said, "Wait for me."

"Right, Boss."

I did take time to thank the nice manager for the four nights' free lodging and to tell him I was off to sea again. Getting back, I just got aboard as the lines came in and we were off down the Delaware River. I never will know if they were really waiting for me, or if they would have sailed without me had I not arrived when I did.

The snow was flying. The deck with ice on it was like a skating rink, making it very treacherous. The lines were nearly frozen and hard to coil. After we battened down the hatches, Boats said, "Go get some sleep, because you go on watch in four hours." I looked back at the lights of Philly and wondered why I had left them for another voyage at sea. "Darn," I thought, suddenly realizing I would miss the party at the Seasons House planned for the next night. It might have been my closest brush with "romance" on the entire trip. Finally I consoled myself by thinking that I was too young—or at least too young looking—for the world of women anyway. The really funny thing was that I didn't even know where we were going. I finally got to ask Boats, "Where are we headed?"

"New Orleans," was his happy reply.

10

Homeward Bound

I was called for watch in time to get a bite to eat before going on at seven PM, and I didn't get off until six AM, just in time for breakfast. The mate hadn't hired anyone to take Ercell's place, so I was the only O.S. aboard. When I first hired on, my watch was eight hours long. That is the standard time a seaman is supposed to be on duty during a twenty-four hour period. Then my watch was changed to nine hours and when we got to Philly, to ten and this time to eleven hours—all night long. When my watch was over I could hardly stand up from being so tired.

One good thing that did happen was that our good bos'n gave me a messman's cabin to myself which was more amidship and more comfortable. I was thankful I didn't have to be in the smoky forecastle any longer. In the bow of the ship, where the crew's quarters were located, one feels every slap of the waves and every pitch of the ship. It was the worst place on ship to try to sleep. In my little cabin I didn't feel that; also, it was nice and warm, even though the weather outside had turned very cold.

We had mostly the same crew as before, except for Erce and a mess-boy who were missing. I talked to some of the crew about what they had done while in Philly and learned that most had spent all their wages on drinks, women, and cigarettes. I think everyone on the ship smoked except me. They were happy to be working again, but I imagined that they would do the same thing when we reached New Orleans.

We went out of Delaware Bay into the Atlantic, but kept close to the coast. I found out why when the ship again came into sheltered waters. We were heading up Chesapeake Bay toward Baltimore, Maryland. Standing lookout on the bow, I reported all lights, but snow fell so hard that it was difficult to see anything. Finally the captain ordered the ship stopped and the hook dropped. The first mate got angry because he had to get out of bed to oversee the operations and when a shackle jammed in the windlass, he gave his crew hell. I was glad to be just the lookout.

We were only about twenty miles south of Baltimore when we finally got anchored. I rang the bell periodically until morning. There were four inches of snow on the deck and icicles a foot long hanging from the boat deck—one above the main deck. I had to keep moving to keep from freezing.

With daylight came clear weather. The ship moved on to pull into a wharf at a large steel mill to load pipe and cables. After that we docked at Baltimore for more freight destined for New Orleans. Everything was white and pretty ashore. I walked up and down the wharf just to be able to say that I had set foot in Maryland. The ship wasn't there long enough for me to do more than that.

After a light truck was lowered into No. 2 hold, the officer on the bridge gave the order, "Standby fore and aft," that meant we were leaving. I helped bring in one line after a stevedore threw it off the dock bollard. We were cleared for New Orleans and standing down Chesapeake Bay. The weather was clear and I stood watch on the bridge with the Captain, D. F. Sargent—also known as the "Skipper" or "Old Man." I thought he was okay because he would talk to me more than any of the mates. Presently a man in civilian clothes came to the bridge and talked to the captain awhile before the Skipper left. The stranger, to me, stayed on the bridge.

"What'er you doing here?" he asked me.

"Lookout."

"All right, keep a sharp eye forward, then." I had been looking at him, because he wasn't too steady on his feet, and I wondered why. I almost asked what he was doing there, but thought better of it. It was a good thing I did, because I found out later he was the new chief mate, having replaced the other one at Baltimore. After awhile I determined that he was under the influence of liquor almost to the point of drunkenness. I think he wasn't too happy about being as- signed to the *Oritani*, so tried to drown his disgust before coming aboard. I had thought he was a passenger, but when Bitterman, the second mate, or Hansen, the third mate, didn't show up on the bridge, I figured that I better be care- ful with the "civilian."

The ship had all of the hatches battened down and ready for sea by three AM. I went off duty at six and I'll tell you, that bunk never felt better. When we got into the Atlantic it was windy and a little rough, but I walked the bridge like an "Old Salt"—a bit proud of myself. It seemed like I had to make lots of coffee for the officers on the bridge, but it was warm in the galley so I didn't mind that. I even had fun watching the salt and pepper shakers sliding back and forth across the table with each roll of the ship. The little railing on the edge of the table kept them from dropping to the deck.

Sunday arrived and with it came a change in the wind. We were now facing a head wind which made the ship pitch more. It also made my stomach pitch more, so I passed up the chicken dinner. We had gotten far enough south that it was warm on deck and too hot below deck. The air was damp and I could smell seaweed at times. Late Monday the wind calmed and I started feeling better and was even eating again. The clouds cleared and a pretty moon appeared out of the southern sky in the direction we were heading.

While on watch with the first mate I asked him why I had to stand an eleven-hour watch while the other seamen stood only eight. He agreed that my watch was too long and he shortened it to, on at 8:00 PM and off at 5:30 AM, although I am sure from the way he spoke, he didn't like doing it. While still nine and a half hours, it was a little better than before.

We were making good time by staying close to the Florida coast. On shore I could see sandy beaches, palm trees and beautiful beach homes about a mile away—near Palm Beach and Miami. One week out of Philly we rounded Key West and headed for the mouth of the Mississippi River across the Gulf of Mexico—in a northwesterly direction. When I brought coffee to the mate while on watch that night, he scowled at me. "What took you so long?" he asked.

"I had to make fresh coffee," I replied.

"Well, hurry it up next time."

"Yes, sir." We didn't use 'sir' much aboard the freighter like would be done on naval vessels, but I emphasized it for his benefit—or maybe for mine. With him I seemed to do everything wrong and nothing right and I was getting plenty tired of shipboard life because of it. My mood seemed to be up and down according to how my stomach felt, and my stomach was more or less regulated by the weather. However, that mate and I never did have a good relationship from the first. To make matters worse, that night a strong northwest wind came up making the sea rough and I started to get sick again as a hard rain pelted my face. That watch seemed to pass slowly. When we had a head-on wind the ship pitched more. I wasn't the only one sick. Two or three others were, and I think the mate didn't feel all that great either. The next night while talking to the captain on the bridge, I said, "I don't think a seaman has a very good life."

"No one with any sense would ever take it up for a life's work. There is nothing to do and no place to do it," he commented.

"Why did you take it up?" I asked.

"When the Depression hit I lost my job ashore and this was all I could get."

Gradually the seas calmed down some and I felt good enough to eat dinner at "souper-time"—as Alec, the mess-boy would say. I had to gain back some lost weight and energy, so I ate heartily for a change.

It took longer than usual to reach the Mississippi River because of the head wind. The helmsman was having a tough time keeping the ship on course and the first mate was giving him "hell" about it. I wasn't the only one he took his wrath out on. When I saw muddy water at sea, I knew we were closing in on the mouth of the river. The dark brown color showed up many miles at sea before we got to the river itself, appearing like a river without banks.

Once we entered the real river the ship steadied and the land looked so peaceful to me along the river banks that it made me anxious to be ashore. It took us all night to reach New Orleans, but I enjoyed my watch while keeping lookout on the bow as we followed along the winding river. When daylight came we were surprised to see a light dusting of snow on the ground—the first snow in that city for many, many years. The newspapers made a big thing of it in their headlines, even though there was only thirteen hundreds of an inch of snow.

Off watch, I washed some of my clothes and hung them

on an iron railing in the fiddley where heat from the ship's boiler would dry them in a hurry. Too excited to go to bed, I went ashore to the post office to see if I had any mail. I was surprised when the man at the General Delivery window handed me six letters from home and a card from Erce. He had been to Buenos Aires, Argentina and to Rosario up the Parana River. I didn't know where that was located, but it sounded exotic. His ship had also stopped at Santos, Brazil. He wrote that they would soon be on their way to Boston, USA. I did miss Erce a great deal and was glad to hear from him. I sent a card off to him to Boston to let him know I had made it back to New Orleans. After that I freshened up by getting a haircut. I could afford the fifteen cents it cost. I also went to the "Y" for a shower and swim. It felt so good to be ashore that I even went window shopping, looking at motor-cycles and other things until it was time for me to get back to the ship.

When I went aboard, Boats took me aside to say, "I am sorry, Kenny, but the mate has fired you. I assure you it's not my doing."

I knew that the new mate and I hadn't gotten along well from the start—and especially after I asked to have my watch shortened—so I wasn't really surprised. "Boats, I'm not un-happy about leaving this ship," I said. "Thanks for being a good friend."

"You can stay aboard tonight and get your pay in the morning," he said.

I ate supper, then turned in because I had been up for thirty hours, so needed the rest. It was a relief to not have to stand watch that night, and I slept solidly for over twelve hours. Had I not been fired, I probably would have quit any-way—especially if the *Oritani* was scheduled to return to Philly, which seemed to be its main cruise. Most of the time I had enjoyed the experience, but once to the East Coast in the winter time was enough I thought.

In the morning, January 26th, I left ship after getting my pay of $14.67 for eleven days work at the rate of $40.00 per month, and didn't even look back at the *Oritani*. I made my way to that wonderful YMCA where I took a room for the night. "Y's" were great because it cost nothing for swimming and swimming suits were unnecessary as we swam nude. The next day, warm and sunny, I spent a lot of time answering my mail—then I had lunch with Max Douglas, a friend Erce and I had made when we were there before.

"You might be able to get a ship to California," he said, "that is if you still want to ship out." I had told him about my experience on the trip to Philly and back.

"That would be okay with me—but I hope it's a better ship than the *Oritani*," I replied, "like twice as large, and with a good first mate."

"I'll work on it," he said as we parted. He had helped Erce and me get our first job.

That afternoon I found and rented a little room near the "Y" for $1.75 a week. It even had a quaint little fireplace in it for heating if it was needed, which was seldom. The furniture was old but the bed had a good mattress. Compared to what I had slept on aboard ship, it was heavenly. The room was on the second floor of an old house and had only one window. I spent most of my spare time elsewhere, so having a better room wasn't as important to me as the price being right—and it was.

Sunday arrived and despite my old clothes I went to church, then walked around the old French quarter (Vieux Carré) of town. Most houses there had balconies with fancy iron railings and grillwork on them. All the windows had shutters. I also visited the Cabildo, built in 1795 as a town hall, jail, and for other city business. It is famous for being the place where the transfer of the Louisiana Territory from Spain to France and from France to the United States took place. It now houses the Louisiana State Museum. I took in a show and felt that I had a very good day.

Tuesday I walked to the Industrial Canal where I checked the Gulf-Pacific Line wharves—but no ships were there. I saw another show, the third in as many days. Afterward I stopped at the public library and started reading *Fiddlers' Green* by Wetjen. It is a fascinating story about legend and lore of the world of seamen. After having been to sea, even if only for a short trip, I had more understanding of how sailors feel and think, therefore the book meant more to me than it otherwise would have. During the days that followed I spent a lot of time at the "Y," where I might play some pool, swim, or watch a basketball game. Sometimes I would go to the library to read awhile before retiring to my little room.

Sunday, February 3rd, I watched the *Point Palmas* of the Gulf-Pacific Line come in and dock. As soon as the gangway came down I went aboard to check with the mate to see if I could get a job. "Come back tomorrow," he said. I did go back and in anticipation of getting on, had my gear with me. I had to wait around most of the day before finally signing on. I feel quite certain that my friend, Max Douglas, had a hand in getting me the job, but I didn't get to see him again to find out. I had been in New Orleans ten enjoyable days, vacationing in the city of the "Mardi Gras" and friendly people, but I was getting "itchy feet" again and I felt glad to have the chance to be moving on again—especially so since it would be to California and on a large ship at least twice the size of the *Oritani*.

Finally, after seven months away, I was homeward bound. The last mail I received included another card from Ercell. It was from Boston, Massachusetts and stated that he would be coming to New Orleans next. I decided to go on to California anyway, even though had I known about it sooner, I would have waited for him. My chance to get another job might not have come as easily.

Homeward Bound

◆ ◆ ◆

The S. S. *Point Palmas* of San Francisco, after the last of its crew staggered aboard drunk, left the wharf at seven PM. The first mate and I handled both lines on the foredeck. He showed me how to take a couple of turns around the barrel of the steam winch and let it do the work of pulling in the heavy hawser. I coiled one line and he coiled the other. We then pulled in the spring lines, the lines running ashore from midship in opposite directions, to hold the ship steady at the dock. The second mate and boatswain handled the lines aft. The crew, in no condition to work, had hit the sack in the forecastle. The mate, different than most, let them stay there while we did their work for them.

During all my time at sea, which included four years as an officer in the U.S. Coast Guard, I never ran into a better officer than the mate of the *Point Palmas*. He was one good one in an ocean of mediocre men. We went through the lock in the Industrial Canal, the same one that Erce and I had portaged around with our canoe. The ship had to be tied up for awhile below the lock until a fog lifted, then we started down the Mississippi River toward the Gulf. The mate and I worked together most all night clearing decks of lines, lowering booms and battening down hatches. At midnight we went to the bridge. "Have you ever handled the wheel of a ship?" he asked.

"Only on a riverboat," I said.

"Relieve the man at the wheel. Follow my directions and you'll do all right," he assured me. We were still in the river, and I was surprised that he would trust me with steering the ship. I remembered that not once had I steered the *Oritani*. I had a little instructions from the man I relieved, then for two hours I did as he told me to do—"Come right a little. Steady as she goes. Come left. A little more. Steady." And so forth. I had to watch the compass closely, because I couldn't see anything else. I didn't have any trouble steering, but was tired by the time another seaman relieved me. The mate told me to turn in for a well deserved rest. He would stay on for another two hours.

I found my way to the forecastle and tumbled into an empty bunk. I didn't get much rest because as the crew was turning out in the morning, they tried, in a friendly way, to get me up, also. Every little while someone would poke me, saying "Turn to, sailor. Don't let the boatswain find you here." They thought I was the worst drunk of the lot, of course, and not doing my duty. Not knowing I had worked a double watch that night, they were, in good faith, trying to keep me from getting in trouble. Most of the crew were young men and good sailors. We got along well together during the voyage, after that first day.

My watch was from twelve to four twice a day—that is, I went on at noon and worked until four, then again at midnight until four AM—four hours on and eight off. I didn't get stuck with any ten or eleven hour watches like on the *Oritani*. The *Point Palmas*, being from the West Coast where the seamen's union was strong, had a crew of all union members, except for me. There were three O.S. seamen and six A.B.'s in the forecastle, which made a full ship's complement.

The weather was warm and calm when we got into the Gulf. I remember the sunset the first night out as being especially beautiful, although we had so many of striking beauty that rating one as better than another became increasingly difficult. One of the pleasures of being at sea was being able to observe the ever changing, immense, 360° sky. Even at night the heavens were star-lit and fascinating, with many constellations prominently displayed. It seemed like our ship floated in a world of its own.

My night watch (early morning) was broken up by various duties so that none became monotonous. I would stand lookout on the bow for an hour, then on the bridge for awhile. At 2:00 AM I would have to oil, then read, the log on the taffrail, and report the numbers to the mate so that he could calculate the distance the ship had traveled since the last reading. He could then determine the ship's approximate position at the time by measuring that distance on a chart in the direction the ship traveled—so much for simple navigation called "dead reckoning." The log consists of a rotator on a long line trailed behind the ship and a recording device on the railing which measures distances traveled at sea.

Then I had a trick at the wheel until time to go off watch. On the *Point Palmas* the officers got their own coffee and didn't insist on being waited on. During the afternoon watch I chipped paint for an hour and a half. We cleaned away the old loose paint so that a new coat of paint would hold better. Then I steered the ship and the mate took a turn at chipping paint—believe it or not. At sea we steered by a compass bearing—which is not very hard to do in a calm sea, but can become very difficult in rough weather, I was told. Perhaps that is why I never got to steer the *Oritani*, because on her we were in rough seas most of the time. In bad seas the man at the helm has to anticipate how the wind and waves will affect the ship's movement and counteract that at the wheel to keep it on course. On the trip to California we had no rough weather at all.

One day the bos'n sent me aloft in a bos'n's chair, a board to sit on suspended by a line, to "whiten the shrouds." A man on deck lowered me as my painting progressed. Some of the men didn't like that job, but it wasn't the first time I had had a job like that. Once when I worked on a sailing yacht I had to sand and varnish a wooden mast 103 feet high. Of course that was in a harbor—but if a speed boat went by it would send me swaying from side to side. I just hung on until the yacht stopped rocking. Boats was pleased that I didn't mind that job, so gave it to me every day until it was completed.

We had beautiful warm days as we neared the Panama

Canal. After dinner those of us off watch sat on a hatch and talked, or just let the sun darken our tans. Most of the sailors' conversations centered around what they had done on their shore leave in New Orleans and what they planned to do in their home port of San Francisco. Most of the crew weren't married, so girl friends were discussed repeatedly.

"Pee Wee, you got a girl friend?" someone wanted to know.

"Naw, I'm too young for that kind of stuff," I joked.

"I'll get you a girl when we get to Frisco," another kindly offered.

"Thanks, maybe I'll take you up on that."

Someone, I think perhaps the mate, had read the story in the New Orleans newspaper about Erce and my canoe trip and had spread the tale. I had already answered quite a few questions about our trip for them, and my name of Pee Wee had just naturally followed me aboard ship. As we sat and talked they asked, "Would you like to make another trip like that?"

"Yes, and I think perhaps I will some day, but I'll do it in the summer time." Some of the younger men thought that they would like to go along, but admitted that they had never been in a canoe.

There was a great deal of difference between how the *Point Palmas* and the *Oritani* were run. As far as I was concerned everything was good on the one and almost everything bad on the other. Of course the good weather helped make me feel better, also.

One day we had fire and lifeboat drill, which involved running water through the hoses and swinging the lifeboats over the side of the ship and back again to their original places. It took only about ten minutes, but was good practice for an emergency.

While I was standing watch on the bridge one star-filled night, the first mate came up to me. "See that bright group of stars south of us," he said, pointing just slightly above the horizon.

"Yes, sir."

"That's the constellation Crux—better known as the Southern Cross."

"Is it above the South Pole?" I asked.

"No. If it was we wouldn't be able to see it from here, but its two bright stars in the longer axis point almost directly to the celestial pole."

It appeared to be a five star cross with four bright stars. That was the first time I had ever seen it, but during World War II I saw it almost nightly for more than a year while cruising in the South Pacific Ocean. It is one of the most conspicuous constellations of the Southern Hemisphere, and once seen, not easily forgotten. We were about 10° of latitude north of the equator at the time.

Sunday, February 10th, was quite hot. We sighted low lying land and trees shortly before dark and arrived off the Panama Canal entrance about nine-thirty to anchor and wait our turn to enter. We could see other ships at anchor, also, waiting to enter the canal. I stood only one hour and twenty minutes of my watch when the mate, being the considerate guy that he was, told me I could turn in. We were anchored about a mile from the town of Colon, Panama. Some of the off-duty crew wanted to go ashore there and asked the mate for permission. "You may take a lifeboat and row ashore," he said, "but be sure to be back for your next watch." That's the kind of guy he was—anything to make the crew happy. They made it to Colon and back in time, reporting having had a joyous time at a bar.

I got up as we started through the canal the next morning, wanting to see as much of it as possible. At Gatun, the first locks, there were three sets of double locks (ships could go both ways at the same time). These raised the ship about eighty-seven feet to Lake Gatun. All the lines to move or hold the ship were handled by black employees of the canal who had come aboard for that purpose. Our ship was towed through the locks by electric locomotives that travel on rails beside the locks. Our crew didn't have to do a thing while in the locks.

After getting out of the last one we slowly cruised through the inland lake and looked at the tropical vegetation, sea birds, and several times spotting crocodiles. We had to go through the nine-mile Culebra Cut before reaching Pedro Miguel Lock where the ship was lowered about thirty feet. Going on through another little lake put us at the two Miraflores Locks which lowered us to the Pacific Ocean level. The forty miles took about ten hours and I enjoyed the entire trip.

Going through the Panama Canal was a great experience for me. At the locks, vendors came aboard selling their wares. I bought a couple of post cards that gave some statistics about the canal that I found interesting. Its construction by the U.S. Government was one of the greatest achievements ever done. The French had started the canal but gave up after losing 50,000 men to malaria, yellow fever and dysentery. The importance of winning the battle against these diseases is largely overlooked when one thinks of the canal, but it was as great as the construction itself. Started in 1904, some 40,000 men worked ten years before the first ship went through the canal. The greatest amount of excavation was done at the Culebra Cut where constant landslides made the work troublesome. Just getting rid of the tremendous amount of soil was extremely difficult. A dam and power plant built at Gatun provided all the electricity needed for the operation of the canal.

The Pacific, living up to its name, was smooth without even a ground swell. We had come 1,441 miles from New Orleans in seven days. By going through the canal, we saved more than 8,000 miles over traveling around Cape Horn—as ships had to before the canal was constructed. We traveled southeast through the canal, so we actually ended up farther east than where we started which seemed rather strange to me, because one thinks of going west through the canal to the Pacific. We were only about 540 miles north of the equator as we left the canal and Panama on the west side. With the hot weather, we forsook the forecastle to sleep on deck in the cooler air of the tropical night. Every day we painted the ship and soon had it looking like new. I also acquired a good tan working at that job without a shirt on. We saw whales, porpoises and a few big skates (flat ray fish) until we got farther north. I would often stand at the bow watching the porpoises swimming ahead of the ship, darting back and forth, sometimes leaping out of the water. That was entertaining, but to see a huge whale break water to "blow" was thrilling.

We skirted the Mexican shore line for several days, seeing long white sandy beaches and beautiful white clouds over the mountains. We had nights filled with moonlight and sunrises and sunsets of crimson glory. The officers seemed more friendly than usual. I think the good weather affected everyone for the better. We didn't work on Sunday and sometimes we would get a stand-by from watch. I had as much as twenty hours off at one time. What a difference from working on the *Oritani*. The food was good and sometimes we had ice cream for dessert. It was better than being on a cruise ship because I got paid for taking the trip. During such good days I would sometimes dream that I might like being a sailor if it could always be like that, but I knew it couldn't.

On February 23rd I sighted Catalina Island, so knew we were getting close to San Pedro harbor—my old stamping grounds where I had worked on yachts and made lots of Sea Scout trips from there to Boy Scout camp on Catalina Island. The mate and I were standing our afternoon watch on the bridge and I kept looking for familiar places.

"Point Firmin dead ahead, sir," I reported as soon as I could be sure of it.

"Well! You must know this port," the mate said in surprise.

"Yes, sir. I've been around that breakwater light a hundred times or more."

"Maybe I should let you take the ship in then," he remarked.

"No thanks. I want to be sure we make it safely," I replied.

When we were docked in San Pedro, I had a delightful surprise. My folks were there to meet me. They had contacted the steamship line to find out when the *Point Palmas* would be coming in so they could be on hand to greet me. Eight months away from home did make us all anxious to see each other. "There's my folks," I said in surprise, more to myself than to anyone.

"Go meet them," the mate said, "and bring them aboard if you like."

I went ashore in a hurry to hug my mother and father, then showed them around the ship—a first-time experience for them. I told them I had signed on to go to San Francisco, but assured them that I would come home from there because I wanted to be with them.

Also there to meet me at San Pedro were two officials from the seamen's union, requesting that I join the union and pay them dues. I knew that the union did the seamen a great deal of good in getting more wages and better conditions aboard ship, but I didn't like being pressured into joining. "I'm going only as far as Frisco," I told them. That didn't seem to satisfy them.

"We will have men there to meet you, and you better join or else."

"Okay, I have to get to work now," I said as I left to go find Boats. I was still on watch. I figured the "or else" meant that I would be roughed up if I didn't join and that they would see to it a union member got my job.

Later that night, after the freight had been taken care of, we left San Pedro to continue on north. Two more days' travel and we entered the Golden Gate of San Francisco Bay —ending a twenty-two day, over 3,000 mile voyage that I thoroughly enjoyed. The *Point Palmas* looked bright and shining. I was proud to have served on her. When Erce and I left Frisco on our bikes, little did I think that I would be coming back on a ship eight months later.

The union "officials" were there to meet me, but it didn't matter because I was leaving the ship. I didn't want to go back to New Orleans on her because I didn't plan to follow the sea as a career. I eventually found a job to my liking in forestry. I took my discharge—on which the captain wrote "ability V.G." (very good), "character V.G.," and "seamanship V.G." The thirty dollars I received for my pay was about twice the money I had when I left home.

The Depression was waning. There were more jobs, and I planned to get one. I was happy to be going home, but I knew I would never stay home for long again. At twenty-one I felt that it was time for me to be on my own. The bumming, vagabond journey was a maturing and learning process for me. I learned that wherever I went people were about the same and mostly good. The trip was a good adventure at the time, but seems to get better as the years go by because I realize that few people have had such an experience. Because they haven't, their lives may be "empty hulls—ships that never sailed." Not that most lives aren't meaningful and worthwhile, but when the time comes to sit by the fire and look back, memories are important, too.

THE BOAT THAT NEVER SAILED

Down in the harbor of Broken Dreams
On the shores of Yesterday,
Her hull half-buried by sands of Time,
A schooner lies rotting away;
And her broken beams are the broken hopes
Of plans that have somehow failed—
And the tide drifts in and the tide drifts out
Past a boat that has never sailed.

Her timbers were made of the finest wood
From the forests of Caribee;
Her sails were like wings of the albatross
That glide o'er the southern sea;
And her decks how they echoed her builder's song
As he fashioned her, plank and nail—
Now only the seagull's lonesome cry
Haunts the boat that has never set sail.

She never answered the siren call
Of coaxing wind and tide;
She never breasted the Spanish Main
With the seas coming over her side;
And the pennant that hangs from her broken mast
Never shook in the lashing gale—
For the tides of Destiny waxed too full
And the schooner never set sail.

Somewhere there are men with snow-white hair
Who sit in life's twilight years,
And often their thoughts drift wistfully back,
And often their eyes fill with tears
As they think of the dreams that have gone astray
And the plans that have somehow failed—
God, heal the hearts of the men who have built
The boats that have never sailed.

—*ALBAN WALL*

A MAN
AND HIS
CANOE

SAILS SHE DOWN SOFTLY

Skidbladner sails,
Erasing time.
Old bones rattling,
Fling of brine.

Sailing again,
Her rigging frayed.
Chill seas under,
Seams unpayed.

Sail into dusk,
May soft winds blow,
Moon light your wake,
Ghostly glow.

Sail you westward,
Over the bar.
Softly, softly,
Avatar.

—ERCELL HART
December 16, 1983

Epilogue

Ercell returned home about a month after I did. At New Orleans, where he arrived from Boston on his last freighter trip, Erce and another fellow bought an old car to drive to California. The car broke down somewhere in Texas, and from there he hitch-hiked to Santa Monica.

I do not know what became of the *Point Palmas* of San Francisco, the 3,048 net ton freighter, but I know a little about the 1,500 net ton *Oritani* of New York. She was built in the Todd Shipyards at Brooklyn, New York in 1921 and christened *Oritani*. In 1939 she was renamed the *Tyee* and operated by Alaska Transportation Company. The United States Navy chartered her and she was commissioned at Puget Sound Navy Yards in 1942—named the U.S.S. *Midway A.G. –41.*

When the Navy wanted to name a new carrier *Midway* (after the World War II battle of Midway), the old *Midway*'s name was changed to *Panay*. The *Oritani / Tyee / Midway / Panay* was decommissioned in 1946 and I don't know what became of her after that. She was only 238 feet long with a 33 foot beam—like I said, small as freighters go.

Before Erce canoed on to his heaven at "Grand Portage," he sent me the following thoughtful words of farewell.

Thanks, Kenny—

When good friends share experiences over a long span of time, they learn to tolerate each other, respect each other, maybe love each other.

Sharing the small boat cockpit, the magic of the quiet canoe, the crispy trout cooking in the pan, the long thoughts around the campfire—these things go to make up the fabric of a friendship that can be recalled for its treasures.

So I count our friendship, one of the worthwhile parts of my life.

Aloha,

Erce

Appendix

HERE ARE SOME POPULAR CANOE AREAS TODAY

Arkansas River
Kansas Department of Wildlife and Parks, 900 Jackson St., Suite 502, Topeka, KS 66612 (913) 296-2281

Edisto River Canoe and Kayak Trail
Box 1763, Walterboro, SC 29488 (803) 549-1035

Ozark National Scenic Riverways
Box 490, Van Buren, MO 63965 (314) 323-4236

Boundary Waters Canoe Area Wilderness
U. S. Forest Service, Superior National Forest, Box 338, Duluth, MN 55801 (218) 720-5440

Little Missouri River
North Dakota Parks and Recreation Department, 1424 W. Century Ave., Ste. 202, Bismarck, ND 58501 (701) 224-4887

Quetico Provincial Park
Atikokan, Ontario, Canada POT 1CO (807) 597-2735

St. Croix National Scenic Riverway
   Box 708, St. Croix Falls, WI 54024 (715) 483-3284

Suwannee River Canoe Trail
   Suwannee River Water Management District
   Rte. 3, Box 64, Live Oak, FL 32060 (904) 362-1001

Willamette River
   Oregon State Parks and Recreation Department
   525 Trade St. SE, Salem, OR 97310 • (503) 378-6305

St. Regis Canoe Area
   New York State Department of Environmental
   Conservation—Forest Protection
   Box 296, Ray Brook, NY 12977 (518) 891-1370

*Historic Upper Missouri River from Fort Benton to Kipp State
Park, through the Missouri Breaks*
   Located in Montana (See page 73.)